NAKED COMMUNICATION

Courageously Create
the Relationships
You *Really* Want

Sage B. Hobbs

RESOURCES:

There are many resources available to make Naked Communication come alive and really work for you and your life. You can explore them all below.

FOLLOW SAGE B. HOBBS
www.sagebhobbs.com
www.facebook.com/sagebhobbs/
www.instagram.com/sagebhobbs/

For Jesse and Dalila, who are my biggest loves in the world,
who challenge me constantly to be a better human
and push all my buttons to make sure I'm still growing.
You are my heart beating outside of my body.

To Nathan, without whom I couldn't do this.
Your unwavering love is my rock.
Your humor makes me happy.

And to my Dad and Gram, whose
love I always feel and
am forever grateful for.

Contents

"When I dare to be powerful—to use my strength in the service of my vision—then it becomes less and less important whether I am afraid."
—Audre Lorde

Introduction

In June of 2011, I put my forehead to touch my dad's forehead and whispered, "I love you, Dad." A single tear slowly fell down his cheek.

For five months he'd courageously dealt with sudden paralysis, adjusting to life in a wheelchair. He watched as his brilliant mind slipped in and out of reality. He confronted, and ultimately gracefully embraced, the rare diagnosis that would end his life. And through the most intense time of his life, he reached out to everyone who'd impacted him over the years. He wrote raw and honest letters that drew people to him, instead of hiding in his own fear and sadness.

In response, there was a parade of letters and visits. I watched and listened as countless people held his hand and retold their memories with my dad. I read letter upon letter written to him in profound gratitude for the contributions he'd made to their lives. I was blown away by the depth of connections my dad had created in his lifetime.

On that afternoon in June, he could no longer speak. A man who'd spent his life teaching and training others around the world was unable to talk. He was close to the end. But, as my head touched his and I tried desperately to convey to him how much I loved and adored him, he heard me. He felt my love.

I communicated. We connected.

And while the sadness at his death was still staggering, he and I both had the profound gift of love being shared. Not just in his final moments, but in my 33 years of being his daughter we were able to really talk in a way that drew us together.

There is one main thing that we all want. At the center of ourselves, when we're being honest, when our ego isn't running the show, and when our basic needs of survival have already been met, we all want one core thing.

We want to have deeply loving, fulfilling, and meaningful relationships with the people in our lives.

In this book you'll learn how to create the relationships you really want. You'll learn how to connect with people more deeply and authentically, from strangers to your most intimate relationships.

When you have the relationships you crave, you'll inherently leave behind a meaningful contribution to the world. You'll have the experience of a life well lived when your final time comes. My dad was an incredible example of this.

I know this to be true, because I want this too, and so do the countless amazing people I've been honored to know and work with.

And I've spent most of my life thinking about, studying, practicing, and teaching how to create and sustain extraordinary relationships. I've geeked out on communication, relationships, human potential, and overall human behavior well before pursuing a career in these areas.

The only thing I've ever found truly fascinating is people. How they think and behave. I talk to them at checkout counters and in the park. I watch them on the street and in their cars. I wonder about their backgrounds and how their lives turned into what they now are. I'm always curious.

Why are some people optimists and others perpetual doomsdayers? What makes conflict easier for some than for others? How do you form amazing and real relationships?

I've had the privilege of working with thousands of people on their patterns, behaviors, and communication styles so that they can restore peace in their relationships, speak up more freely, form more intimate connections in their lives, and generally cultivate their relationship skills. Thus, they become happier and more effective in their lives.

So, how do you create deep, meaningful, intimate relationships in your life?

You become masterful at naked communication.

Communication is based on so much more than the words we use in a moment of interaction with someone. Our communication is based on everything we've ever experienced—our childhood, our education, our influences, how our parents spoke to us, the stories we believe to be true about our lives.

Our communication is complex. It is full of many automatic patterns that we're often unaware of because they feel like such a part of who we are. Before we can relearn to communicate effectively we must strip away all these layers and find ourselves as we originally were: naked and open to limitless potential.

This book will take you through the process of stripping away all the layers that confuse and muddle your communication, and then teach you the tools for clean, clear, compassionate, and *courageous* communication. Naked communication.

When you've peeled back the layers and begin from a clean slate, you can create all of your relationships through this new way of relating, the "naked" way. It requires vulnerability and courage but is insanely effective in getting you the relationships you want.

If you're reading this book, you're already totally amazing! I know this because you're here, reading. You're choosing curiosity. You have a desire to grow in your communication and relationships.

I'm guessing you're reading this for one of the following reasons:

You want to be able to build relationships that make you happy.

You want to strengthen, invigorate, or repair the relationships you're already in.

You want to be able to effectively and confidently ask for what you want.

You want to experience less guilt and more freedom in how you relate to others.

You want people in your life to feel valued and appreciated when they're with you.

You want to be courageous and clear when you are speaking with others.

You want others to be inspired by you and what you have to contribute to the world.

This book is meant to be inspirational, wildly useful, and fun. Because that's how I aim to live my life, and I wanted to write my book accordingly. The useful part is essential because inspiration without action won't get you the results you desire. (That's also why there's a hands-on book guide to support you at www.sagebhobbs.com/bookguide).

Recently, I had the profoundly fabulous experience of seeing Bruce Springsteen perform live with my mother. Bruce (as he's called in our home) has been a part of my life since childhood. Fist pumping through the open sunroof, my mom would cry out the words to "Badlands" while taking us on whatever weekend errand we were up to. Then she'd tell us about his spirit, his politics, his passion, and (of course) his "hot" backside in those jeans.

A few decades have passed since the weekends in the car with my mom, but Bruce is still an active part of our family lore. So, when we all went to see him (my sister, husband, stepdad, and stepsister as well), I was ready to have a good time.

What I wasn't fully prepared for was the fact that I would cry for half of the show. I cried because the energy in the arena was palpable. Because Bruce was so clearly pouring his soul into the audience. Because he shared stories of his life that were so real and honest. And, mainly, because I felt connected to him somehow, and so did the many others around me. He managed to create connection with thousands and to make me feel so deeply ALIVE.

I know none of us is Bruce Springsteen, and most of us will not find ourselves in an arena of thousands (though some of you may!) But, what I want for you is the ability to form connections, to feel intimacy, and to relate to others with as much ease as possible. Even in a massive room full of strangers, there was an opportunity for human connection that Bruce utilized. It felt like he shared an experience with all of us, in a way that was relatable and intimate. And in sharing his energy, spirit, and heart in such a real and honest way, I felt lit up and inspired myself.

I want you to feel inspired. Powerfully able to create connections in your life. Lit up by the idea of asking for what you truly want. Knowing that you deserve a life you love, and a life that matters. Confident that you can express yourself effectively with anyone in your life. Courageous enough to go for it. And, you don't have to be Bruce Springsteen for this to be possible.

Bruce is 66 years old. His energy, vitality, humility, and love at that concert (and at every concert he performs) was mind-blowing. It's important to remember, though, that he was once an awkward teenager from Jersey who just wanted to play guitar and write songs. His ability to connect evolved over time, as can yours.

Naked communication is about stripping down the way you've been doing things in your relationships, and in all of your communication, so that you can start from a completely fresh space. From that nakedness, and with the strategies included here, you can create the relationships you really want.

It's likely you were drawn to this book because there's something else that you want in your life. You want to explore, create, cultivate, and nourish connection. You want something deeper, something greater than what you have now, a completely new and wildly refreshing way of approaching your relationships.

I'm going to walk you through the best ways that I know to communicate powerfully and honestly ("naked"), so that you create an extraordinary life, with loving and connected relationships that leave a lasting mark on your heart and the world.

In the book's three sections I'll help you reflect on where you are now, prepare you for new and better possibilities to come, and then give you the tools to start using naked communication to actually build the relationships you want. I'll give you examples, stories of both successes and failures, that will help to deepen your understanding of the communication principles I lay out for you.

If you're already checking out, thinking to yourself, "She doesn't know *my* family. She's never met *my* husband. They'll never change" or, "My relationships are fine. I'm a good communicator already," I invite you to keep reading anyway. There is always an opportunity to take your relationships, and therefore your life, to the next level of greatness.

Throughout the book there will be questions and prompts to guide you through this transformational discussion, to help you strip down your patterns and reinvent how you connect with others. I encourage you to actually pause to consider them and apply them to your own life. Don't pause so long that you get stuck, struggling to answer them and then don't finish the book. You can always return to them later. But if you can consider them as you read along, you'll be able to integrate the ideas of naked communication into your life right away.

Transformation comes from inspiration AND participation.

Most of us have some relationships that work smoothly and others that challenge us. In both cases, we've often given up on changing them. We take for granted the ones that are working and forget that we could add a new level of depth. With the ones that drive us crazy, we're often resigned to "the way things are."

What if it were possible to communicate so that you could cause instant connection with anyone, anywhere, at any time?
How would it feel to go through your life knowing that you could handle the conflicts that arise (which they inevitably do) with confidence and grace?
What if you could feel more love and affinity with the people in your life?
More laughter and honesty with your friends?
More courage and confidence in making requests?
Less guilt and fear when asking for what you want?

All of this is possible for you when you work on naked communication.

At the risk of sounding like a ridiculous optimist (which I shamelessly am), I believe that naked communication is an essential global conversation. I wrote this book at a time when the news was filled with acts of violence that stem from lack of connection, from people more interested in being right than being happy, from misunderstandings and non-listening.

I know the world is complicated. It's full of differing opinions, belief systems, ways of life, values, and needs. There is no simple fix to the struggles that we're facing.

Yet, so much starts with a conversation. Between *human beings*. Whether they're neighbors or country delegates, their abilities to communicate in a way that fosters connection instead of distancing is where it all begins.

As each of you builds your skills in naked communication, and thus your ability to connect with *everyone* in your life more meaningfully, the impact on the world is huge. From your own personal world to the world at large, YOU are a part of a bigger conversation.

At the core of everything, it's all about human beings and how we connect. Relationships are the bottom line, the pulse of the human experience.

Let's do this.

Part 1: The Here and Now

We're going to dig in, and dive deep, to become masterful at naked communication so you can really build the relationships you want. Don't worry, you can keep your clothes on, but you do have to strip away many layers of your old habits.

First, let's start with where you are, with your current understanding of communication, so we can then begin to look at it through a new lens. This is how you've probably thought of communication for most of your life—that is, if you've given it any conscious thought at all (which many haven't).

According to Merriam-Webster, *communication* is:
"The act or process of using words, sounds, signs, or behaviors to express or exchange information or to express your ideas, thoughts, feelings, etc., to someone else"
Connection is defined as:
"Something that joins or connects two or more things"

I define naked communication as:

"An entirely new paradigm for relating to yourself and others. It requires stripping away old habits so that you are in a more vulnerable and naked state. It is courageous, clean, clear, and compassionate. Its purpose is to deepen the connection in all of your relationships, so you can have the love and fulfillment you crave."

It's really not as hard as we think it is to build happy relationships. We screw it up all the time because we're stuck in automatic patterns that we've never given much thought to. Most of us haven't been taught how to build relationships well. If we're lucky, we've had a few good models in our life, but mostly we're figuring it out as we go, leaving a mess of lost opportunities and subpar relationships in our wake.

In this section, you'll reveal what *your* patterns of communication are, and how they came to be, so you can transform them into ones that truly serve you and your relationships. New and naked are waiting for you.

Chapter 1: We're *always* communicating something

We're all communicating all the time. You've heard this before, from the way you move your hands to the way you hold your body. From what you say, to what you hold back from saying. From the tone of your voice to the clothes that you're wearing. From your text messages to your Facebook posts.

And then, of course, there are the actual words that come out of your mouth. Words are extraordinarily powerful. They can elevate, wound, create, transform, and heal.

In order to be more masterful in your communication, so you can consistently communicate in a way that brings you greater connection, fulfillment, and happiness, you've got to first get clear on how you already communicate.

When I was growing up my family "fought" openly. Not often, but when we did it was understood by all involved that there was a conflict. Sometimes I didn't even think of it as fighting so much as working things out and then making up. If my mom was pissed or frustrated, we knew exactly why because she would tell us. Sometimes she'd tell us more loudly than we'd like to hear it, but at least we always knew where she was coming from.

If things got heated, as they did more often when I was a teenager, we'd yell. My mom and I are both fiery and passionate. These traits serve us well when leveraged toward doing meaningful work and keeping the spark alive in our intimate relationships. We make things happen. We bring fun and energy to our relationships.

However, these characteristics could be explosive when we disagreed, had our feelings hurt, or in some way found ourselves in conflict.

But, we always worked it out. We talked it through, listened to the other's point of view, owned our part, and apologized authentically. (I'll talk more about cleaning up messes later. It's a skill we all need to practice.) To this day, I can (and do) communicate openly and honestly with my mom. I know we can work out our issues compassionately as they arise, even if it gets heated.

You might say my communication style is assertive and open.

Fast-forward a couple of decades, and I've just moved in with my now husband.

We have fundamentally different views of conflict that we've had to work out. To put it in simple terms, I believe that conflict happens, it's natural, it's okay, and it gets resolved. He believes that conflict is uncomfortable, not good, doesn't always end well, and should be avoided unless absolutely necessary.

So our first fights went something like this...

I'd be irritated over something relatively small, like the cabinets always being left open, and I'd bring it up calmly. He wouldn't think it was a big deal, and would want to avoid the discomfort of an "issue," so he'd simply try to change topics or dismiss it somehow. I'd get more angry because I didn't feel heard.

He'd feel confused about why I was getting angrier over something so trivial and again try to move us away from the topic or say a quick apology and "move on." I'd get increasingly irritated that he couldn't simply understand and acknowledge my frustration about the cabinets, so I'd escalate the conflict to be about him not understanding me. He'd get even more confused because he thought we were simply arguing about open cabinets. And on and on it went.

His communication style could be described as passive and conflict avoidant, also described as "chill" or relaxed.

Obviously, this caused some tension in our relationship. We couldn't understand each other's styles, and neither of us felt good about how our conflicts played out. I'd sometimes let my thoughts go wild and begin to question the entire foundation of our relationship. "He'll never fully understand me. He can't handle little challenges; what happens when something that's really hard comes up?" I felt vulnerable and scared because I couldn't fully see how we'd learn to communicate better, and yet I knew I deeply loved him and wanted our relationship to work.

Now, more than a decade into our relationship and a couple of kids to up the ante, we've really learned how to respond to each other much more effectively. In order for that to happen, we had to be curious about what the other person was feeling, what they really needed, and be patient with each other. We also kept returning to how much we loved and respected each other, so that our differences didn't outweigh our commitment to our relationship.

Do we still have conflicts? Of course. You'll hear about some of them in other parts of the book.

Do we both default to our long-time communication styles? Yes, but not as often.

Most importantly, we understand each other and our needs better. We don't have fights that damage the core, foundational love of our relationship.

Until we had an understanding of how we each tend to communicate, it was easy for us to fall into conflict. Once we examined our own communication patterns and behaviors, there was space to create our relationship in a way that worked best for both of us and for the partnership itself.

Every one of us is constantly communicating *something*.

Be a curious observer of how *you* are constantly communicating.

For a full day, notice all of the ways you communicate.

Text messages. Emails. Phone calls. Social media.
Conversations with your kids, your partner, your colleagues, clients, friends, strangers.
How you carry yourself at work, at home, on the bus.
The pace of your walk. The position of your shoulders.
The volume and tone of your voice.
The words you use, or don't use. Do you say "sorry" or drop the F-bomb regularly?
The clothes you wear. (Yep, they communicate too, whether we like it or not.)
Your eye contact. Your handshake.

We live in a world of near constant communication, yet we struggle with deep connection. The more you can recognize all the ways you communicate every day and in every moment, the better chance you'll have to strip it down and consciously choose what will work better.

Chapter 2: Your communication M.O. How are *you* currently communicating?

I'm a "straight shooter" most of the time. Very often this approach to communication serves me well. People know they can trust me to be honest. They know I will let them know if I'm upset or have a concern, and that I'll stick around long enough to work it out in a way that feels good to both of us, as much as possible.

Other times, being a direct communicator has gotten me into trouble. I've hurt people's feelings, or offended them, by speaking too quickly without giving enough consideration for how my suggestions or opinions would make them feel.

For example, when I was 22 years old I had my first "real" job and I was fired up about it. I had a million ideas about how to support kids and make change within the Philadelphia Public School system. This was no small task for a district that had been chronically underperforming for decades and was riddled with challenges.

I would sit in meetings with bright, committed, and hardworking women who were my superiors in both age and leadership experience. Since I'm a straight shooter, and extremely passionate, I'd openly share my ideas, offer suggestions, and give my feedback.

After a few months in my new, shiny, exciting job I was called in for a meeting with a couple of these powerful women. My bosses.

I can't remember the exact words they used, but what I heard was that I needed to tone it down. I was being too brazen with my suggestions. I seemed like an overly eager, young, white (Philadelphia schools and much of their leadership were predominantly African American) know-it-all. Basically, "Who the hell do you think you are? You've got to slow your roll," was what I heard.

I was absolutely mortified. It was the exact opposite effect that I'd hoped to have. I wanted to bring in upbeat optimism and create lasting change, not piss off a whole bunch of women whom I admired and respected.

It was a momentous growth opportunity for me. I called my dad, who was a masterful communicator, connector, and coach, for some advice. He guided me to apologize for any offense I may have caused, take responsibility for how my excitement was misinterpreted, and make a request to partner with them and work collaboratively on our shared desire to help kids.

It was one of the scariest and most courageous conversations I'd ever had at that point in my life. And, because of it, I forged much deeper connections than would have been possible before, when I was unaware of how my communication style impacted others.

These women whom I'd initially rubbed the wrong way became my mentors, and I learned a ton from them throughout my time in that role. Those connections wouldn't have been possible if they hadn't given me the gift they did, which was to communicate with me about how I could express myself more effectively and humbly.

You have to consider the myriad ways that you already communicate. Not just in conflicts, though that's a key area, but in expressing love, offering your ideas, and making requests.

Ask yourself the following questions to deepen your understanding of your own communication habits and to see more clearly what your communication style is.

How do you approach conflicts? Do you meet them head on, wait until they are too glaring to avoid, or something in between?

Do you fight mean or fair? Do you bring in months or years of past evidence to fling at them? Or do you directly share why you're upset and make clear requests about how to resolve the problem?

Do you express your love and appreciation openly and generously? Or assume that others "know how you feel about them?" How much, and how often, do you really let others know what they mean to you?

When your friends are making dinner plans, how do you express your desire for the restaurant or time that works for you? Do you go with the flow, and end up resentful, eating Korean barbecue at midnight when you're an early bird vegetarian?

When your boss asks for feedback on a new project or initiative, how do you contribute (or not) your ideas? Willingly, fearfully, confidently, hesitantly?

When the cashier at the checkout line asks how your day is going, how do you respond? Passively, honestly, reciprocally?

These questions help you get at some core communication styles. Think about which ones of the following apply to you. Be honest with yourself here—no one's reading over your shoulder! Remember, the clearer you are about your own communication, the better you'll be at building awesome relationships.

Confrontational/Avoidant
Assertive/Passive
Confident/Timid

Direct/Subtle
Demonstrative/Withholding
Exuberant/Restrained

None of these are bad, and none means that you're a terrible communicator. You just want to know yourself and strive for growth and balance. If you're like me, and you tend to be direct, you may need to consider when that's appropriate and when it ticks people off. I'm also super demonstrative. I love to show love and affection, which most of the time works out well. However, my kids would sometimes appreciate if I didn't smother them in kisses so publicly and yell out my devotions so loudly. Knowing yourself leads to growth and balance.

All day, every day, you are communicating. We have countless conversations a day, as well as texts, emails, posts, body language, etc. By looking at how you deal with different opportunities to communicate, you will start to see a pattern emerge that shows you some of your communication habits or tendencies.

We get a million messages about how to communicate and be in our relationships. It can be extremely confusing. I'll give you a list of some of the countless messages you may have received throughout your life. You can check off those that were commonplace in your household or community. Really notice how you've ingrained these messages as "truths" and consider how they have had a profound impact on how you connect, or struggle to connect, with others today.

"Sweep it under the rug."

"Wait until it blows over."

"Actions speak louder than words."

"Sticks and stones will break your bones, but names will never hurt you."

"Just walk away."

"Stand up for yourself."

"You don't want to step on toes."

"Don't let people walk all over you."

"Chin up."

"Speak up already."

"It was just a joke."

"Don't let 'em see you cry."

"Get over it."

And a particular favorite to say to girls: "If you don't have anything nice to say, don't say anything at all."

Are there others that were family mantras in your childhood? Take a minute to write them down.

The magic in this exercise is this: These are just words, not "truths." You can *choose* to adopt them when they serve and inspire you, or let them go when they're bullshit and keep you disconnected.

What's critical is to observe yourself and identify how *you* are currently communicating with everyone around you.

How you communicate directly impacts how you show up in the world around you.

How does your communication make people perceive you at home, at work, in your community, with your friends? Is you communication powerful, insightful, confident, shy, nervous, distant?

Why is this so important to this conversation?

Because we must know how we already function so we can identify the areas that are working well, and the areas that are not, when it comes to strengthening our ability to *connect.*

Relationships are the foundation of everything in our lives, from our family to our work to our happiness. Truly. And connection is at the heart of relationships.

Yes, money, time, sex, career, laughter, books, movies, health, and adventure all sound great too. But without the relationships that celebrate, encourage, and participate in those other aspirations they are meaningless.

The happiness and fulfillment you seek doesn't exist in a vacuum. It lives in relationship with others.

I've talked to countless women, and many men, about their challenges and dreams. The common thread is the universal desire to have deeply loving, meaningful, and fulfilling relationships. The access to those types of relationships is *connection*. Naked communication is simply the tool for connection. Connection is the juice, the meat, the heart of it.

Chapter 3: What do you really want to say? A common pitfall.

Now that you've begun to identify your communication patterns, the automatic way you do and say things, let's look at a common pitfall. One of the things people do all the time is skirt around what they really want to say, what they really need, or how they really feel. It's avoiding the hard conversations that require courage and vulnerability.

This is something we've all been guilty of, for various reasons that I will address later. But I want to bring it up here because now you've begun to take the blinders off of your own communication habits, and you'll start to have more choice and freedom about how you communicate. With that freedom, you'll begin to notice places where you have dissonance, where things aren't quite working right.

Let me give you an example:

I was sitting in my office across from a distraught mom of a teenage boy. They were always fighting. She couldn't reach him anymore. She didn't know what was happening to him or why he was always so angry with her.

She gave me the example of their usual morning. He's getting ready to leave for school, dressed in his "skater look," ripped-up jeans hanging low, boxers visible to the world, beat-up sneakers, hoodie.

"Pull up your pants," she says. He rolls his eyes. "Don't give me attitude first thing in the morning." Another eye roll. "Really, you look like a bum." He turns away. Mom's voice raises. Son retreats further into his hoodie and wants to get away from her as quickly as possible.

Now mom's in tears in the school counseling office, wondering what happened to her sweet boy.

My question, "What are you *really* trying to tell him?"

Because it's not about the jeans. The jeans alone don't make you this sad and upset.

The answer, "I'm scared he's getting into drugs and he'll go down the wrong path like I did and I don't want him to suffer that way. I'm terrified."

Here's the thing: We often spend a lot of time and energy fighting, talking, criticizing and nitpicking without addressing the actual issue that's bothering us.

It's a super common communication challenge. This lovely mom, who adored her son, was struggling to speak honestly about what she really wanted him to know.

That she loved him. That she had made mistakes when she was his age that had caused her a lot of suffering. That she wanted him to be safe. That he could trust her and talk to her about his life.

Instead, she constantly picked fights with him over seemingly unimportant things, such as his clothes.

As you can imagine, this created the opposite outcome to what she desired. Instead of an open and connected relationship with her son, he wanted nothing to do with her and thought she was a total pain in the ass. Lose-lose situation.

So, I ask you... What are you really trying to communicate with the people in your life?

Look at what is getting in your way of the honest communication just below the surface that wants to be expressed.

You're pissed at your partner for coming home 30 minutes late again, so you pick a fight about dinner.

In fact, you want to say, "I really want you home when you say you'll be home because I need to know I can trust you to do what you say you will."

You want to work on a really cool new project at work, but so far you haven't been added to the project's team. So, you keep gossiping with colleagues about the project's design flaws, or that the development schedule isn't right.

Instead, you want to say to your boss, "I have some ideas that I think could be really relevant to this project. Could we meet to discuss them?"

Usually there's underlying communication we haven't expressed when we're fighting about the same things again and again. Or when we're gossiping with the people who have no power to effect the change we desire.

I know sometimes we don't even realize we're doing it. And, I know it's scary to be honest and clear.

I also know that effective communication fuels more connected relationships.

And more connected relationships make us happier and more fulfilled.

And being happier and more fulfilled is where it's at, right? We all want to feel good.

Next time you find yourself nitpicking at your kid, your husband, your co-worker… ask yourself, **"Is there something else I'm really trying to say here?"**

And then, with compassion and courage, say what you mean.

I promise you, as you improve your naked communication skills, your relationships will grow and evolve. And your happiness will too.

Yes, shit will hit the fan at times. Challenges will show up. You'll find yourself hooked in your old patterns of communicating. You'll walk away from an interaction and kick yourself because you know you didn't handle it nakedly.

That's fine. That's normal! Go back to what I share in this book and keep practicing. No one nails their communication every time. No one. But, you become masterful at naked communication so that you can truly *cause* the connections you desire with all the different types of people in your life.

Chapter 4: How do *you* listen?

We've talked about how you communicate your own ideas, thoughts, and feelings. How you listen is equally, if not more, important to communication and relationship mastery, yet it is probably one of the most challenging aspects of communication. We humans really struggle to actually be present with others, not distracted by our own thoughts or waiting our turn to talk.

We also listen through muddled ears, but we don't realize we're doing it. Muddled listening is when we bring in all of our preconceived notions, beliefs, or opinions about someone when we're listening to them so that we can't hear them clearly.

In naked communication, you take off your earmuffs that screw up your ability to listen clearly so that you can hear the people in your life from a fresh and open perspective. This transforms how present you can truly be with them, gives them a better opportunity to actually be heard by you, and allows you to form stronger connections.

And here's something you may have never thought of before: You listen to each person in your life differently. Some people in your life never even stand a chance of you hearing them clearly. You've unknowingly written them off years ago.

This might sound crazy, but it's critically important. Here's an example. Your mother is always nagging you. No matter how successful you are or how well you're doing in life, she's always asking questions that seem to make you "prove" it to her. Every time you call her, the conversation sounds exactly the same. And you're always irritated and disappointed by how it goes.

You're convinced that she's just an "unhappy, never satisfied pain in the ass." Therefore she can't sound any other way because you are convinced that "that's just the way she is." When you listen to her, you have her boxed in by your idea of who she is. You can't hear anything else.

When your listening is clouded by your rigid ideas of who people are, you lose the chance for deep, naked connection.

I don't know your mother, but I do know that your experience of her is your truth. But your truth is just an interpretation, and in this case it's hindering your ability to feel love and affection for your mom.

It may not be your mother, of course. You can substitute any person here that comes to mind. The more connected the relationship, the more likely you have built up a way that you hear them that is really rigid.

This is only a problem when it impacts your love and affinity with them. If you always hear someone in your life, like your partner, as loving and supportive, that may serve your relationship beautifully.

But I want you to look at the relationships you have where there is resentment or a lack of depth that you crave. In those relationships where there's a struggle, there's likely a way that you always hear that person. You have a fixed way of listening to them.

So what do you do about it?

Unfortunately, you can't change another person's personality or way of being unless they have a desire for their own change. When I was a counselor I used to tell my students all the time, "The only person's behavior you can control is your own." They didn't always like that feedback, but they understood it. They could see that having others stop gossiping wasn't in their control, but that they didn't have to participate in it.

While you can't fundamentally change who others are, you *can* change how you see them in the world. You *can* change how you listen to them. You *can* change your rigid or stuck perception of them.

When you change these things, you have the power to shift the entire dynamic. It is enormously freeing. It can return a lot of love into some of your most challenging relationships.

You make this change by deciding to listen from love, acceptance, and a blank slate.

As with everything in the book, this part of naked communication takes practice. It's an old and ingrained pattern when you've listened to someone a certain way for years or decades of your life. However, each moment you're in a conversation with that person, you can choose to love them for who they are, even when you don't always like it. You can choose to listen with clean ears, and an openness to the conversation being new or different, like a blank, or naked, slate.

I have talked to so many people who have felt an entirely new level of love and connection in their relationships when they tried this. It's as if the other person literally doesn't sound the way they've always heard them. The exact same sentences and words may be coming out of their mouth, but they just don't sound the same anymore.

Let's go back to the mother example, because I know that mother stuff comes up for a lot of people. Instead of simply hearing your mother as totally nagging and annoying, let's replace the magnifying glass of negative and patterned thinking with, "My mother always loves me. She's proud of me and what I do, even if she doesn't know how to express it."

When you can reframe the way you hear someone, and be open to hearing them from a fresh perspective, it reopens the possibility of strengthening that relationship.

I know this can be really hard sometimes! I know there are people in your life where you might feel it's impossible. Try it out and look for some evidence to help deepen your belief about it. Maybe she shares all of your creative ideas with her friends and you know that that's her way of talking about how proud she is of you. She always answers the phone when you call and you know that's her way of being there for you and showing her love. She asks all of her damn questions because she's a worrier and she wants to make sure you're okay.

Instead of your mother being a nag, she may sound loving or interested in your life.
Instead of your son sounding lazy, he may sound like simply a searching teenager.
Instead of your husband sounding boring, he may sound steady and calming.

Another way to transform your listening in more strained relationships is to find something you like about that person. It sounds so simple, but it's so powerful.

For example, my husband's a teacher at a big public high school in our community. We run into his current and former students all over town, and he is deeply beloved. Mostly he enjoys the adolescents he works with, but every year there are a few who drive him nuts and push his buttons. The same was true for me when I was a school counselor. We always remind each other to find something to like about each student or person we work with. It immediately casts that challenging person in a fresh light.

This works remarkably well even in our most intimate relationships. Just like within ourselves, we tend to see our flaws and shortcomings more often than we see our strengths and positive attributes. With others we allow their challenging parts to show up louder in our world, and it totally disrupts our ability to connect more deeply with them.

So, let's say your husband is often late, leaves his towel on the floor, or doesn't express his love and appreciation as much as you'd like. These things drive you crazy. And, he's incredibly fun-loving and makes you laugh. He's a hard worker and always gets things done. He's loving and playful with the kids. He's creative and up for adventure.

We are whole, complicated, multi-faceted beings. Your husband can drive you nuts, and you can still choose to focus on some of the things you like about him. When you have something you like about the other person more clearly positioned in your mind and you show up to a conversation with them with love and the possibility of a blank slate, you can hear them differently.

Now remember, they may never fundamentally change. They might, but only if that's of their choosing. However, when you change how you hear them you can change how you experience the relationship.

Sometimes I've talked with people who really have a lot of evidence of hardships, suffering, neglect, or wrongdoing with people in their lives. They struggle to get to a place of a blank slate and love. If this is you, I understand. And, it's still possible for you to have a shift in those relationships.

I'll talk about forgiveness, and how it's for you, not them, later in the book. For now, there is a sentence that helps a lot. I deeply believe it to be true after years of working with some of the most troubling situations and family dynamics.

It is, "They're doing the best they can with the skills they have."

This does not excuse the ways people have hurt you. What it does is frame how you listen to them differently, so that you have the opportunity to interact with them in a way that brings you greater peace and happiness.

They did the best they could with the skills they had.

Sometimes people's skills are limited. They didn't have a good example of love from their own mom or dad. They felt so wounded and insecure that they didn't know how to show up confidently as a parent. They can't be open and vulnerable because they were always told to "man up" and "stop crying." They're scared to love fully because they've been hurt before. They gossip because they never learned how to effectively resolve conflicts.

They have the skills they have, and they did the best they could with those skills.

So you could be asking yourself, "Well why the hell didn't they go get better skills?" You might be thinking that's what you would do and that's what they should've done. Yes, maybe. However, they didn't. And like I said before, you can't change what they choose to do or not do. If you want to restore some of the quality of your relationships, it's you (in this case, how you listen) that must change.

Remember, you don't have to do any of this. You can choose to let things be as they are. But you're reading this book because you want to have relationships, you want to connect deeply and lovingly with others. To love and connect is a courageous act.

Why bother with the people that are hard and who aren't going to change?

Because *you're* drained and exhausted by holding on to anger, resentment, and hurt.

When you change how *you* listen, you get to feel more free. You lighten the load of those negative feelings that weigh you down. You have more energy to put toward creating the relationships you really want when you're not burdened by the relationships that are exhausting you.

I know some relationships may always have their challenges. Relationships can be messy. For example, sometimes it might feel nearly impossible to hear your ex-husband with love or to find something to like about him. Sometimes you get triggered, you feel hurt, you want to just run from that person.

While there may be periods in a relationship that challenge you deeply, it's about letting go of the negative energy so you have more room to build and improve your relationships as much as possible. You shift the dynamic in the relationship by the way that you listen to them, so that *you* have more freedom and space in your life. This may be a kindness to them, but the gift is really to you, your happiness, and your freedom.

Chapter 5: Know your triggers: What pisses you off?

The last piece to understanding your own communication patterns, so you can step into naked communication, is to know your triggers.

All of us have things that set us off. Sometimes it's the "little" things like not closing the kitchen cabinets. Not putting the milk back in the refrigerator. Not picking up socks from the living room floor.

These seemingly "little" things might set you off into a yelling rage or into a silent, passive- aggressive, pissed-off morning. Whatever the "uglier" side of your communication style is, it comes out when you get triggered.

There are also the "bigger" triggers, which can be harder to identify. These may be the underlying traits or behaviors that are based on your past experiences and therefore they set you off big time. It's your responsibility to know what these things are so you can manage your communication, and thus your relationships, accordingly.

For the past several years, our family has taken a 5,000-mile road trip with our kids. Almost every day is something new and fun with family or friends. We go to the beach, the Franklin Institute in Philadelphia, children's museums, swimming pools, have junk food galore, and watch lots of movies. For the kids it's *the* most fun thing in the entire world. They look forward to it every year and have a blast.

However, inevitably, there are moments when I lose my shit because I feel like they're not grateful. I feel like they expect every moment to be awesome. It can seem that they're not being helpful and cooperative while we're managing a lot to make this trip happen.

This past summer our typically sweet and loving seven-year-old son asked me a question about when we would be going on our annual day to the boardwalk. I don't even remember exactly what he said, but I was triggered. All of my alarms were going off about entitlement, spoiled brats, and ungrateful people. I go big on this trigger. My mind starts spiraling into the privilege we have in our country and our affluence compared to the rest of the world. I go down the rabbit hole of anger, frustration, and blame. And on this day, my son heard my wrath and got a lecture on gratitude and appreciation.

I have a major trigger about entitlement.

Even the example of leaving socks on the living room floor can get my entitlement trigger ramped up. I can find myself yelling, "Why can't you just pick up your damn socks? Why does everyone assume I'll take care of it? You need to take care of your stuff! Not everyone has enough socks in the world! Do you want to buy your own socks?"

I can go crazy with the entitlement trigger, as my family will tell you.

Of course I have my reasons for why this upsets me so much. And my reasons may be valid. But it doesn't mean that they serve the quality of my relationships and my ability to communicate effectively with those in my life.

Triggers usually unleash a part of us that isn't quite in control. When we're triggered we react with less thought and consideration. This is why it's essential to know what you're triggered by, so you can anticipate them and respond in a way that truly serves you and those in your life.

What are *your* triggers?
Remember, inspiration without action won't get you the relationships you want.

List as many of your triggers as you can, from the "little" to the "big."

Now think for a moment…

How do you respond to each of these triggers?

Do you yell and scream?

Do you shut down?

Do you go away and disappear from the other person?

Do you dissolve into tears, unable to be consoled?

Is your response different depending on who triggers you?

The more you can understand your triggers and your reactions to those triggers, the better you'll be able to master naked communication to deepen your relationships.

There's nothing wrong with having triggers. Everyone has them. Those who have identified their triggers, and dug deeper into the impact they have on their lives, have far more ability to cultivate the connections they desire because they know how they themselves react and respond to their triggers. They can tread lightly on the trigger landmines of life, practicing how to respond mindfully and not simply react mind*less*ly.

Part 2: Preparing You for New Possibilities

Before I can fully teach you how to be a naked communicator (which I will, I promise), we have to explore a few more pieces of the puzzle. You are much more likely to actually practice and integrate naked communication into your life when you see:

- What it could make possible for you and your relationships
- What is holding you back and tripping you up
- What the costs are in your own life to maintaining the status quo

For example, if someone told you to stop eating sugar completely and to instead drink green smoothies, but didn't tell you the amazing health benefits that could be possible from the change, there's no way you (or any other sane, chocolate loving individual) would listen. If I taught you how to write the most incredible and captivating keynote speech ever, but didn't address your sheer terror about delivering it, then the speech would be a waste. And there's no way my husband would have given up good beer and bread if the he didn't feel the pain of Celiac disease ravaging his gut when he consumed them.

This section is all about understanding what else is possible in your life and relationships that inspires and excites you. It's about learning what is holding you back, and how to bust through it, so you can attain those fresh possibilities. And it's about really getting the cost, the loss, or the suffering that will occur if you don't make a change, so that you have the fuel to make this courageous shift into naked communication.

Chapter 6: Because something else IS possible for you and your life

I was talking to Debbie about a new man in her life. She'd been divorced and had since been looking for a deeply connected and passionate new relationship. Debbie had no problem getting dates. Men were drawn to her.

The challenge arose in attracting the men that she really desired. She kept finding herself with playful, life-of-the-party types. While they were fun, they couldn't give her what she really wanted.

Debbie was ready for something else. On some level she knew it was possible to meet a different kind of man, but she wasn't sure how to go about it.

We really dug into how she perceived herself, what she truly wanted, and why she deserved to have it. Debbie is incredibly smart, creative, talented, and passionate. She's interested in personal growth, adventure, and creating a meaningful life. She's successful in her career and has tons of friends.

Debbie wanted a man who was on a similar path of success and self-discovery. But, first she had to BELIEVE that it was even possible to find a man like that. She had to believe in the possibility of creating new patterns and communicating a different message out in the dating world.

Once she saw that something else was possible for her and the men she attracted, she started taking different action. She expressed herself more honestly on dates. She told her friends and peers about her creative projects. She said no to men who weren't a fit for the new possibility she'd envisioned. Different types of men started to show up in her life. Smart, creative, supportive men who were psyched about her ideas and passions.

Okay, don't roll your eyes here. Stay with me. The reason you picked up this book is likely because on some level you're really hoping that something else is possible for you and your life too. This is what Debbie discovered, and there's something for you to uncover for your own life as well.

Perhaps it's better girlfriends whom you feel really supported by, instead of judging and comparing.
Or a relationship with your mother that doesn't end in an argument with every phone call.
Or a loving, intimate relationship where you feel appreciated, connected, passionate.
Or to stop feeling so damn guilty when you say NO.

Or to feel free to ask for what you want, without worrying about hurting people's feelings.

Or to be seen as someone who is up to cool stuff in the world, because you're more able to talk about it.

Or the ability to go to an event or party and feel more comfortable talking with people.

Or to share yourself more easily so your relationships are deeper.

The list is endless. Relationships are at the heart of every part of our day. From the grocery store to the CEO's office, you're communicating and creating relationships.

We get so stuck in how we see the world and how we express ourselves. Our blinders are on, but we don't realize it. This tunnel vision screws everything up.

In the next chapter you'll learn a fundamental principle that will change everything about how you see the world and relate to others. But first, you have to entertain the idea that something else, something better, is actually possible.

Debbie started to see how she was worthy of what she longed for in a partner. She began to really get that the fun, playful, flirty side of her was only a fraction of her big, beautiful, brilliant self. She didn't have to let that old story go entirely. She could maintain her fun-loving identity. But she could also make room for the possibility of her deeper side.

When she did, she began to date completely different men. She found herself in a relationship with a creative, smart, and supportive man who wasn't threatened by who she was and, in fact, found her compelling and bright.

It was amazing to watch her transformation as she embraced all the possibilities available to her with a fresh perspective. She also got an incredible new job with many more like-minded creatives who supported her skills and wanted her to thrive. She moved into a new apartment that was way more aligned with her vision of a "home."

Something else IS possible for you and your life. I promise.

You DO have to read the book, practice, take risks, get support, be willing to grow, and believe that something else is possible for you (even if you can't quite see the forest through the trees yet).

Let's look at an example from someone who's now extremely successful, and seemingly happy, but wasn't always that way.

Tony Robbins is one of the world's most renowned transformational leaders. He's worked with people like Oprah and Bill Clinton. He has a multi-million-dollar company that offers programs and services to make people's lives and businesses better.

He has an incredible story, in which you can see how simply changing the "story" changed everything. The messages he'd received as a kid weren't serving him well. Like all of us, he thought those messages were simply reality, until he received a different message and was able to see an entirely new possibility about life.

As a kid, he lived in poverty. His parents divorced when he was seven, and his mother began abusing drugs and alcohol. He described his household as chaotic and abusive. He had a step-father who communicated a message like, "You have to look out for yourself because no one is going to help you out."

However, there was a holiday in his childhood that changed Tony's worldview, that offered him a different "story." A stranger knocked on his family's door and gave them a holiday meal. For free. No questions asked, no expectations of returning the generosity.

Tony was blown away by this act of kindness. Not simply because it was food and they needed it, but because someone else DID care about him. *People could be thoughtful and helpful, just because they chose to be.* The message that people only looked out for themselves was blown apart, and a new possibility opened up.

This would be a radical concept to a child who had previously lived in the "story" of "look out for yourself because no one else will." It rewrote the possibility of reality.

Tony Robbins has gone on to have a hugely impactful career of service, and has included feeding families who are hungry as his philanthropic outreach.

Now, I don't know Tony Robbins personally. I'm sure, just like all of us, he's had his challenges in his relationships and in the ways that he communicates with the people in his life.

But, his story is a great example that something else is possible. That you can be a child in poverty, with abuse and messages of hopelessness surrounding you, and still find your way into the idea that life could be different than what you had believed. That you can be the one to master the skills needed to transform your relationships and your life.

This is WHY I wrote this book. More importantly, this is why YOU are reading it (I hope!). Because you're hoping something else is possible for you, and you're brave enough to explore what it might be. Communicating for true connection is the path to the relationships, happiness, and fulfillment that you desire. When you do this, the ripple effect in the world is profound.

You might be thinking, "That's great, Sage, but I'm not Tony Robbins. You don't know my family. They're nuts. What if it just isn't possible for me?"

I hear you. I've heard countless people in my life have reservations about the ability for things to change. I happen to be a bit of a possibility junkie. I've studied it, I've practiced it, and I've worked with many others to broaden their ideas about what is possible in their lives.

I'll give you many examples throughout this book of real people and real lives. You have to be willing to expand your thinking *just enough* to let in an ounce more of possibility than you had before. When you have the opening of possibility, coupled with the skills of naked communication that I lay out here, you really have a combination for change. You have a much greater opportunity to transform your ability to communicate effectively and cultivate deeper relationships.

One of my clients, Kerry, contacted me in the throes of a life transition. She was miserable in her job, just out of another breakup, and feeling down on herself in general. She was the mom of three happy, well-adjusted teens. She'd managed to build a career for herself while raising her kids and going through a divorce. She'd been courageous enough to put herself back onto the dating scene, even though it was scary and new to her. She was full of life and humor and had a resiliency that was admirable.

However, she didn't see all of these awesome attributes about herself when we first began working together. She'd lost her connection to her own greatness. She knew some part of her was a capable and talented designer. She understood intellectually that she was fun-loving and upbeat and attractive. But, she wasn't feeling it.

Kerry was too wrapped up in her story of "things don't work out for me." She had a long history of believing that things simply didn't go her way. Every time something didn't work out as she planned, like her marriage or her most recent relationship or her job, it became further evidence for her story that "things don't work out for me."

Our work together helped her to see that the story "things don't work out for me" was made up and was really messing with her happiness. Through much courage and bold action, Kerry was able to see that something else was possible for her and that SHE held the power to change her story.

And she did.

She got a new job where the staff adores her and her work. They value her as an essential member of their company. In fact, she received an unexpected financial bonus for her stellar work, along with accolades from her boss.

Kerry also brought fun back into her life. One of her primary goals was to take better care of herself, be more playful, and create more fun. She reached out to friends more often, joined activities that made her happy, and practiced saying no to things that she really didn't want to do.

Kerry's a caretaker, as I'm sure some of you reading this book are as well. She was in the habit of always putting others first and "never having time" for herself. She's a single mom who placed her kids' needs before her own.

She's very proud of her kids and how she's parented them, as she should be. But now, she gets to have her own happiness as well. The entire family gets a say in what they need and want, which really serves everyone better. The kids get to see that it's possible to make changes in your life to be happier. What better lesson is there?

I recently saw Kerry at one of my presentations. As we were catching up, I was blown away by how she created a completely new possibility for herself. The possibility of being a loving mom, who also takes care of herself and rocks at her career.

Kerry is amazing, and she's just like all of you. She was stuck and couldn't see what was holding her back. She wanted something else but couldn't quite see the possibilities.

But, she was willing to explore, to learn, and to go for it. She learned new ways to communicate with her boss, her kids, and herself. She made a commitment to create more connection with her friends, and then took the steps necessary to make that happen.

Chapter 7: What's your story? Fact vs. fiction

You can't transform your relationships, and your ability to connect with others meaningfully, until you're clear on a fundamental concept.

It's an idea that changes everything. And for naked communication to work, so that you can have stellar relationships, you'll want to really go for it in this section. You'll want to engage with this idea in your life. I guarantee you, when you live your life with this belief, it can change everything. It's that powerful.

Much of what you believe to be true is actually just made up.

Said differently, we are fabulous story tellers who are so damn convincing that we've led ourselves to believe our reality is based on fact.

Or, most bluntly, we make shit up. All of us do it all of the time. Literally, we are always placing our interpretations onto our experiences, but we act like those interpretations are true. They feel true to us, until we can see more clearly, more naked.

This is human behavior—to make meaning of our lives and our circumstances. However, when we accept, and really begin to believe, that there are infinite interpretations to any situation, we then have powerful choices in how we live, love, work, create.

When my son was five years old he wanted to take his bike to the awesome new bike park. It was the last day of spring break, and we'd promised him we'd take him before he went back to school.

My husband and son, his buddy and his mom, and our neighbor loaded up the car, and off they went for a final spring break adventure.

About an hour later my phone rang. "Meet us at the emergency room. Jesse fell off his bike." Shit.

I passed my two-year-old off to a neighbor and headed to the hospital, where I found my sweet boy swollen, crying, and bleeding profusely. Next to him was my loving husband, drenched in blood from using his shirt to suppress the bleeding. It was quite a scene.

Several hours later we headed home with eight stitches inside Jesse's mouth and the medical equivalent of crazy glue on his upper lip. We stopped for a milkshake to ease his misery and to give him some sustenance in liquid form. It dribbled all down his chin because he was so swollen he couldn't suck. He looked like a puffer fish that'd been in a brawl.

Here's what happened that day: He rode a loop at the bike park that had an elevated wooden ramp without incident. When he rode it the second time he fell off. He split the inside of his lower lip and the outside of his upper lip. He got eight stitches in his mouth and surgical glue to his lip. We got a milkshake and went home. These are the facts.

Now here are some of the infinite interpretations of that incident, the "storytelling" possibilities he could have told himself:

I was going too fast and was out of control. I should be more careful. I wasn't paying attention. My dad screwed up and took me on something too challenging. Bikes are scary and dangerous. I suck at riding a bike, never doing that again. My parents were irresponsible and stupid to take me there. I wasn't ready. I'm not going to ride a bike anymore because it's too risky. Life's too scary to take risks.

Or, he could have drawn these conclusions:

I'm so brave and hard core. I rode so fast and it was awesome. I love adventures, even when they get a little wild. I'm totally going to master that loop next time. My dad's so cool for taking me to do fun and crazy stuff. I was doing really well, but I just had an accident. It could've happened to anyone. The doctors were so nice and it hurt, but not too badly. I need to get a better bike so I have more control next time.

Every single thing that happens to us we can interpret many different ways. We can choose interpretations that serve us well, or not, in terms of how we live our lives.

I chose this incident as my first example for a reason. Things happen to us early in life, before we're five years old, and we interpret the incidents from that childhood state. There's nothing bad or wrong about doing that, it's simply automatic.

Where it can become damaging and hold us back from the love, happiness, and fulfillment that we desire is when we continue to believe it's true and find evidence that we're right about that "truth" throughout our lives.

My son went on to ride over 250 miles to and from school that year. He told the accident story with a bit of pride to his friends. He doesn't want to ride the loop again, but he still loves to go on adventures with his dad and trusts that his dad doesn't put him at risk.

You can see that if he'd decided he was clumsy, and kept living as if that were true, he'd miss out on learning to ski, riding his bike, canoe trips, sports on the playground, and much more. Instead, he decided it was just an accident, and he's free to explore life as he grows up without the burden of "I'm clumsy" or "life's too scary to take risks."

This is essential to the beliefs you have about yourself. *Consider that "who you are" might be based on the stories you've been telling yourself.* For example, if you were the new kid at school in first grade, and you subconsciously decided "I don't fit in," are you still living like that's a truth? Do you show up at a party feeling awkward and uncomfortable before you've even entered the room?

With my clients, I can see through their stories to their strengths. Kerry believed "things don't work out for me." I saw resilience, courage, and competency. I saw the story "you always make things work." My story was just a story too, but one that filled her with possibility instead of exhausting her.

If you're still not convinced about this idea of fact vs. fiction, I invite you to consider it and notice all the thoughts that go through your head in a day. You'll be amazed at how convinced you are that your thoughts are true. When you can begin to realize that they're really just your interpretations, your world blows wide open.

Another of my clients transformed from "I'm ugly and different" to "I'm beautiful and desirable" once she could see how her childhood stories were just bullshit. She wore glasses. She had darker skin. Her parents spoke another language. Those are the facts. The rest, she could rewrite.

When I was thirteen years old my parents gathered us into the living room. We never hung out in the living room. It was the most formal room in our 125-year-old Victorian house and it was rarely used, so I knew something wasn't right.

I was in the throes of appropriate teenage self-absorption, trying to make it through middle school unscathed. I was used to a steady, mostly happy, childhood. My brother was nine and my baby sister was just two.

"We're separating," they said. I literally didn't understand. They never fought. We went on family vacations. They threw parties with their friends. Separating?

I knew that parents got divorced. I knew that existed in the world. Just not in my world. And in that moment my world grew bigger and a new reality began to take shape.

This was my first moment when I realized that nothing in life is a guarantee. But again, that was my INTERPRETATION. At that time, I didn't know it was just a story I'd made up about the divorce. But I've since seen the ways in which that story, which I perceived as true, has impacted my life.

Sometimes that "truth" has empowered me and served me well. In my twenties I traveled to more than twenty countries. I met amazing people, tried new things, learned a ton. I've always felt like "Nothing's a guarantee, so I'd better not wait to do what I want and make things happen."

Other times, that story has disempowered me and made me fearful. When I was 23 I was diagnosed with cancer. While I was appropriately shocked and terrified, it also supported my story that "nothing is a guarantee." Surviving didn't feel like a guarantee. This story from a decade earlier in my life evoked more fear in my cancer diagnosis initially.

I was deeply fortunate to already have done a lot of transformational and personal development work, so I didn't stay stuck in that story. I could see that it was a story and it wasn't working for me at that junction in my life. I was able to identify different interpretations that served me more as I underwent treatment.

I chose interpretations that empowered me instead of terrified me. I told myself how lucky I was to have access to amazing health care. I told myself that if others could get through cancer, then I could too. I told myself that I could be beautiful without hair. I told myself that I had the most loving and supportive friends and family in the world.

Not all of the stories were easy to believe at every moment of my cancer experience, of course. Finding hair on your pillow and feeling nauseous aren't fun, and felt scary at times.

But, the facts were that I had Hodgkin's lymphoma. That I needed chemotherapy and radiation. That the data showed a likelihood of survival and a small chance of death.

The rest was up to my interpretations and the stories I chose to tell myself.

Naked communication is a way to deepen connections with the people in your life. Even the people with whom you've had conflict. You know, the ones you've been pissed at for a while. The ones you don't like, but have to "deal with."

However, you've got to embrace this idea that your reality is simply an interpretation. That there are infinite interpretations to anything that happens. Ultimately, that you're not always right.

You don't have to agree with the actions or opinions of others. But, if you want to connect more meaningfully, you must be willing to consider that what you believe may not be "true."

I'll refer to this foundational idea throughout the book again and again because it's *that important*. It's the magic sauce. When you can see that so many of your conflicts, your suffering, and your crap relationships have to do with actually believing your personal interpretations are true, a million new possibilities for love and connection open up to you.

Chapter 8: What would be possible in *your* life?

Examples are great, but really, this is about YOU. What are you longing for in your relationships? What are you quietly wishing and hoping will shift? Naked communication *is the path to that possibility.*

Right now, I want you to pause and actually dig into it a bit with the following questions:

What would be possible for you and your life if you began using naked communication to deepen your connections, listen more clearly, ask more openly...

- With your partner?
- With your boss?
- With your friends?
- With your kids?
- With your co-workers?
- With yourself?

If you could make requests freely, what would you ask for and from whom?

Who would you reach out to if you were able to honestly share your love and appreciation (even if it's scary to be that vulnerable)?

Who would you clean things up with, forgive, or confront if you knew that you could handle conflicts with grace (even if you can't control the outcome)?

What would be possible in your love life? Your sex life?

What would be possible for your creativity and passions?

As you start to answer these questions, to explore what else might be possible, you'll notice that your old interpretations and stories get LOUD. You might resist really going for it because you hear things like:

"This is ridiculous, that could never happen."
"He'd never say yes."
"I could never ask for that."
"Sounds good, but she doesn't know my mother."
"I'm already pretty good at communication, with the people who listen."
"It'll hurt their feelings if I say that."
"I don't want to step on toes or ask for too much."
"I feel guilty even thinking about it."

Remember, these are all messages based on old stories. They may or may not be true.

As these thoughts come up, ask yourself, "How is this serving me?" If the answer is that it's not serving you, that it's keeping you stuck, that it's making you feel small or unimportant or lonely, then let it go.

Choose a different interpretation or a different story to tell yourself. And keep reading. You'll learn much more about what holds you back and how to move forward in future sections of the book.

Chapter 9: Being right vs. Being happy

"I finally found Mr. Right.
I just didn't realize his first name was Always."
—Sunday comic on our fridge in my childhood

Somewhere along my own exploration, training, and personal growth path I came up against this key question:

"Do you want to be right, or do you want to be happy?"

This usually poses the very first challenge when you start exploring "fact vs. fiction" in your life. Your mind battles against the idea of infinite interpretations because it so much wants to be right, to believe that the reality you've been living is "fact." That others are wrong.

Human beings LOVE to be right.

We want to be right for many reasons. It feels good. It feels safe. It's what we know and believe, so it's scary to consider other views, ideas, or interpretations. It's satisfying when others are wrong (a hard one to admit, but it's often the case).

But, being right can be a lonely hill to die on, my friend. I can argue with the best of them (and have), but a fierce determination to be right, to prove your point, to "share" your opinion can lead to mega unhappiness and loads of disconnection with the people around you.

I'm desperately trying to teach this idea to my kids. The other day my kids were happily playing when they got into a discussion about where the stuffed otter came from. Grandma's house or a trip to the aquarium?

Their fun, happy, *connected* playtime quickly dissolved into a screaming match about where the damn otter came from. The desire to be right is like a hardwired habit that we have to consciously push back against if we want to be happy and stay connected.

In the world of naked communication, it's a simple choice that you make again and again.

"How will being right in this conversation, or this conflict, deepen your relationship?"

When you ask yourself this question throughout your many conversations, you'll begin to see how often the need to be right gets in your way. Sometimes it feels like both people are just talking *at* each other, no one's listening, and each is desperately racing to the finish line of "being right." Along the way, the relationship erodes and you're left feeling less connected.

I had a client who came to me because she wanted to heal her marriage. Her husband had had an affair and she felt deeply betrayed and hurt. Unsurprisingly, their connection was weakened and they were working to restore love and trust. It was a raw and painful time for them, and they were striving to figure out how to move forward.

I offer this example because most people will jump to a similar conclusion when they read it. She was right and he was wrong. He shouldn't have cheated. He shouldn't have jeopardized his relationships with his wife and kids. It's so easy to fight for the "rightness" in things like infidelity. It feels so right to be right about it.

The thing is, it doesn't matter if she's "right" or not. Proving that she's right, arguing about it, and making her point will not restore the love, friendship, and connection in their marriage. And, ultimately, that renewed connection is what she *really* wants, much more than simply being right.

She stretched herself courageously to reopen her heart and be vulnerable, to let go of being right and making him wrong, and to recognize how she could contribute to the rebuilding of their partnership.

It took peeling back layers of old stories and interpretations. It took catching herself in her patterns again and again. It took being "naked" and raw and real, even though it was scary as hell. It took letting go of being right in order to choose to be happy.

When she did this she opened up the *possibility* of renewed love and partnership; that option was closed when she could only see how right she was. Her courage and her choices created the opportunity to rebuild something awesome that they shared. She's a total badass.

She's a total badass who didn't always see herself as one. In fact, one of the first things we focused on was building the belief of "I'm stronger than I think I am." I could see so much evidence of her courage, but she struggled to own that powerful and strong part of herself. In many ways, it would have been so much easier to stay stuck in being right. She would have had no problem getting agreement and support from her friends and family. People are quick to agree that infidelity is wrong.

However, she wanted her marriage and her loving family intact more than she wanted to be right. So she had to set aside being right, as well as struggle with the two other things that hold us back in our relationships, which I share with you in the next section.

She's a total badass, courageously choosing happiness over righteousness.

Chapter 10: What's stopping you from having the relationships you want?

This is the big question. What the hell trips us up or holds us back from creating the depth of relationships we desire?

You're obviously smart, capable, and amazing because here you are reading this book, willing to grow and evolve. You're also clearly an action taker because you're still reading and, hopefully, answering the questions and doing the exercises. (I also created a free book guide to help you follow through at www.sagebhobbs.com/bookguide). Remember, inspiration without action won't get you the results you want.

So, why do so many of us screw up when it comes to communication?

Why is it so hard to build and sustain the relationships we want?

There are two reasons why we suck at communication and struggle in our relationships. These two things govern so many of our choices, and hugely impact our natural ability to meaningfully connect.

These two Achilles heels are…fear and lack of self-worth. These nasty little shits show up throughout our lives at every turn. They look and sound slightly different to each of you, but their impact is the same. They hold you back from creating what you want, in relationships and beyond.

I'll get into the details of what they are, how they present themselves, and what to do about them so you can bust through to a new level of awareness and freedom. The good news is, like anything, when you take the blinders off and can see clearly, you can choose to change your patterns and create the happiness and fulfillment you desire.

That's the whole point, right? To be able to connect deeply with others and have relationships that feel good to all involved.

Chapter 11: Fear

As *New York Times* best-selling author Elizabeth Gilbert said in an interview, "The only people I know who are fearless are toddlers and sociopaths. And I don't want to model my life after either of them." As a counselor, I worked with a few sociopaths. As a mom, I've raised a couple of toddlers. And I'm with Elizabeth; I'm not aspiring to follow their example.

Fear and courage have fascinated me for as long as I can remember. As a cancer survivor, world traveler, and loud-talking extrovert, I've often been described as confident and fearless.

Yet, I've been a bit of a worry wort since childhood, and have worked hard to not let anxiety rule my life. It escalated after my cancer battle in my early twenties, when I struggled with debilitating panic attacks that left me feeling ashamed for being "weak" or "needy."

After my cancer treatment was over, I left my "professional" job in Philadelphia to move to Boulder, Colorado, and regroup with one of my best friends from college. I wanted to tone down my ambition in a beautiful place with a slower pace.

I was volunteering with an awesome organization for teens and working at a coffee shop in the public library. I was riding my bike and doing yoga. Making new friends and going camping. My hair was growing back, my body felt strong, and it seemed like everything was turning out beautifully.

Then one afternoon I was standing behind the counter at work, looking out over the gorgeous creek that flowed under the enclosed bridge where the cafe sat, smiling at the three customers in line and jotting down an order. I was the only one working and wanted to be friendly and efficient, as always. Even then, I loved connecting with customers and learned much about their lives in our two-minute interactions.

On this particular day, out of nowhere, I lost my breath. I was sure I couldn't breathe. Literally, as if my lungs would no longer fill with air. The backs of my hands tingled. My palms were sweating. I thought I was going to throw up. "I must be dying," I thought, "or something is terribly wrong with me."

I politely excused myself and quickly got to the bathroom. Splashing water on my face and sitting on the cool tile floor, I struggled to breathe evenly and calm myself down. I felt terrified and utterly confused.

I learned afterward that I had experienced a massive panic attack. I felt mortified. I'd traveled to Africa, survived cancer, moved across the country. What the hell was wrong with me that I was experiencing debilitating fear?

To me this fear meant I wasn't the brave, confident, and independent woman people thought I was. I worried that I wouldn't be able to have the big adventurous life I'd hoped for.

I felt discouraged and like a fraud. The world saw me one way, while I was secretly waging an internal battle against fear.

But, as I began to study fear and examine the world around me more closely, I realized that fear is everywhere. From my mentors to my friends to my family to celebrities, we've shared this experience.

I've read that Warren Buffett, the billionaire investor, was terrified of public speaking.

Abraham Lincoln is reported to have struggled with severe anxiety.

And actor Emma Stone has had panic attacks since she was a kid.

I live in an adventurous town of über athletes, who appear to be able to scale walls in a single bound or run for 24 hours straight over mountain passes, but I'd bet each one of them has thoughts like:

What if I fail? What if they don't like me? What if I look like an idiot?

So how does fear play out in our relationships and communication? Here are some of the most common ways it shows up in our daily thoughts. Notice which ones are familiar to you:

What if I upset him, or step on his toes? Maybe it's not worth the risk.

What if I ask for what I want, and she says "no?" I'll be so embarrassed.

I don't want to offend people or hurt their feelings.

I don't want to disappoint them or let them down.

And the big whopper… What if I fail, look like an idiot, or feel stupid?

We are often ruled by how we appear to others. Mostly, we want to look good and avoid looking bad.

Any of these could happen. In fact, you've probably already experienced failure, hurting someone's feelings, disappointment, and myriad other fear-related incidents in your life. *And you survived.*

Aiming to be fearless is useless. Fear happens. And, in many ways, that's a good thing.

Fear can indicate that we're standing on the edge of something exciting. A new opportunity. A new adventure. A new relationship. If you're *not* experiencing any fear (highly unlikely), you really have to examine if your life is as fulfilled and connected as you want it to be. Are you playing it so safe that you're never faced with opportunities to try something new (which can be scary)?

Fear is a universal human experience. Perhaps there are the rare few who've mastered their fear (Superman?), but mostly, we all have moments when we're scared.

I struggle with fear every single day. Most people would never know that about me. Anxious thoughts creep into my head at any given moment. As I was writing this book, fear showed up again and again about what it'll be like to share this work with the world with my name attached to it. Will people like it? Will they find it valuable? Will I have left a grammatical error?

When it comes to naked communication, and how you create depth and connection in your relationships, fear trips you up.

Naked communication requires a lot of vulnerability. It's scary as hell to honestly share your feelings, desires, and fears with others. Very often, you're just too scared to do it, so you keep your relationships at a surface level that feels safe. But love can't exist in a vacuum. Depth can't happen without sharing who you really are.

Brené Brown, a leading researcher on vulnerability and shame, put it brilliantly: "Embracing our vulnerabilities is risky but not nearly as dangerous as giving up on love and belonging and joy.

I was working with a client who felt like she had very little support in her life (an old story she was carrying around.) In reality, she was surrounded by many people who would like to know her better, both old friends and newer acquaintances. We started exploring what it would feel like to have an awesome community of support, of people she could call upon when things were stressful or when she wanted to celebrate something.

Before she could even envision the joy of that support system, she was bowled over by fear. She was terrified of being let down, disappointed, or abandoned if she really let people in. She was also scared that her seemingly perfect life would appear a myth if she shared any of her struggles.

She worked hard to move through the fear and take steps toward deeper friendships. Initially, it was really uncomfortable for her. With me, she was so real, raw, loving, and courageous. I knew that others would see that too if she let them.

Here's the thing: no one likes to tell their shit to a "perfect" person because no one wants to look bad. If you're using all your energy, and avoiding your fear, to appear like you've got it all together it's very hard for others to connect with you. When you can be "naked" and more honest than it may be comfortable to be, you'll start to connect more deeply.

Staying safe is the most human thing in the world. Our brains are actually a mechanism for safety. On a primal level, we're animals who are hardwired to survive, so when we experience fear our brains naturally shift into the fight or flight response. And vulnerability can bring up a ton of fear. When that happens in your relationships you have a pattern of response to either fight or flight, or a combination of both.

Fight can look like nitpicking, insisting on being right, proving your point, going for their weaknesses, bringing up past shit again and again.

Flight can look like avoiding conflict, leaving the relationship when things feel too good or bad (both can be scary), pulling your love away by denying sex or physical affection, or checking out mentally.

When fear is running the show, the opportunity for depth in your relationships is screwed before you've even had a chance. Your fear will stop you in order to offer a sense of safety.

I was having a drink with a dear friend and fellow coach who had just gotten remarried. She is wildly in love and has been smiling like a crazy lady since she met this person. She's never been happier. She's never felt anything like this before. All of those fairytale-like feelings.

She's also a total badass. She runs a successful business, is outgoing, dynamic, tall, and beautiful. She appears to be a force of nature in many ways.

Yet, she was sitting with me talking about how, since the wedding, her fears were coming up big time in this new, amazing partnership. Since moving into a new home, she'd found tokens from her partner's earlier life adventures. An old photo. A book with an inscription. Her fear kicked in. She found herself wanting extra affirmation from her partner and promises of security. She caught herself on the edge of picking fights, stopping herself before she unnecessarily caused a rift in their connection.

I looked at her and said something like, "Being in love is one of the biggest risks we take. It requires sharing ourselves in the deepest way. And there are no guarantees. But you know it's worth it, even though it's scary."

While feeling love can be an experience of great safety and security, it also has the flip side of fear. Fear of losing the love.

We go about our lives, communicating constantly, faced with endless opportunities to deepen our relationships, but our fear often holds us back.

So, how do you deal with fear?

Many books have been written about how to manage fear. I'll give you my simplest answer, to this not-so-simple challenge called fear.

I *choose* courage over fear. And I have to make that choice over and over and over again.

I once heard an interview with a very successful businesswoman who said, "I have more fear of regret than I have fear of failure." This resonated with me deeply. I want to live a fulfilling life, and relationships are at the very core of a life worth living. When I think of fear of regret being bigger than other fears, it helps me to take risks. It helps me to be vulnerable so that I may be rewarded with greater depth and connection.

When you choose courage over fear, you have the opportunity to look at how fear holds you back and keeps you stuck. You ask yourself the questions that interrupt your patterns and keep you committed to naked communication and the relationships you love.

Here are some questions you can ask yourself in order to interrupt your automatic patterns. These questions will help you be more naked in your communication. They will remind you that you're *more* committed to building relationships you love than staying stuck in fear.

"What do you really want?"
"What else is possible in your life?"
"What difference are you here to make?"
"What do you want to model for your kids?"
"What do you want your relationships to feel like?"
"Who, if anyone, can you share your struggles with?"
"Who do you call when you need a boost?"
"Do you want to die surrounded by those who truly know and love you?"

Choosing courage over fear means hearing the fear talk in your head, but not letting it take hold. Write the book you've always had in you. Share your hurt feelings with a friend. Ask for help on something you don't understand. Tell your husband you want more romance. Give a talk in front of a bigger audience. Go to the party where you only know a few people because you want to make new friends.

I recognize my fear, but I don't let it take control. I don't let it be the primary factor in my decisions. **My desire for love and connection is the primary factor behind my actions.**

I notice my fear-based thoughts with curiosity. I don't ignore them. That would be utterly impossible. But I don't let them run the damn show. I aim to let them pass by, without attaching to them for the ride. I don't want to be carried away by the fear thoughts.

My relationships are worth the risk. And so are yours.

Chapter 12: Self-worth

"It is of practical value to learn to like yourself.
Since you must spend so much time with yourself you might as
well get some satisfaction out of the relationship."
—Norman Vincent Peale

Questioning our worth is the second reason that we struggle with our relationships. For some of you, this is the primary thing that gets in your way. I wish I could simply tell you that you are worthy. Because you absolutely are. I wish you would just believe me when I said you deserve to be happy and loved. Because you totally do.

But *you have to feel* this self-worth for yourself, which is trickier, but absolutely possible.

I was on a coaching call with Leanne. By most accounts, Leanne would be considered beautiful, smart, and successful. She's highly educated, with degrees from top universities. She has a handsome husband and two adorable children. She has a career that supports environmental philanthropy and has ascended the ranks within her field.

We were deep in discussion about saying no more often, making requests that would help her feel more balanced, and generally working on how she could have her life run more smoothly. She constantly overcommitted in order to feel valued, prove her worth, look good, and not disappoint people. The result of being such an "overachiever" was feeling like she was doing a half-assed job everywhere and really overwhelmed on top of that. We had to break through her story of constantly needing to prove her worth so she could see her amazing strengths and values clearly.

Mid-conversation, Leanne paused to ask me, "Do any of the women you work with really feel confident?" I laughed, and replied something like, "Yes and no." Much like Leanne, the women I've had the honor to coach have times when they feel confident, clear, and worthy. They also have times when they feel doubt, fear, or the old habit of pleasing others first.

Even those who seem to have it "all together," like Leanne, have their old stories dragging behind them like anvils, leading them to question their worth in some way, at some point in time.

In The Big Leap, Gay Hendricks talks about his theory of the "upper limit problem," hypothesizing that we humans struggle with how good we'll allow our lives to get. The theory is, the better our life gets, the more uncomfortable we feel because we don't believe we deserve it. We often sabotage the awesomeness, the success, the happiness because we doubt our self-worth.

These are not new concepts, but they're critical for you to pay attention to if you want to deepen your connections and have more meaningful relationships. For example, if on some level you're not sure whether you deserve a passionate, supportive, and loving romantic relationship it's going to be harder to create one. Not impossible, because someone might be able to crack open your heart and help you see your own worth, but mostly you have to believe in yourself first.

When I was leading a Women's Circle program, issues of worth came up every time we met. This group of bright, loving, capable women would courageously gather to connect and talk honestly about their lives.

Initially, I'd facilitate the conversation with a mindfulness practice and then a discussion question or prompt to get the ball rolling. This was an essential starting point because, as I've mentioned, sharing ourselves honestly can bring up a lot of fear.

However, as time passed, the women opened up with each other, and an outpouring of stories, laughter, and tears ensued every time we met. Remember, our desire to connect is innate; we just have to listen to it and keep our fears and doubts out of the way.

One evening, as we sat in a circle eating and settling in, Taylor mentioned how hard it was for her to get to our group because she felt so guilty leaving her kids at bedtime.

She felt like it stressed her husband out and disappointed her kids. She felt so guilty that she should be at home helping out, but she also felt like she really wanted (and needed) her own time away. Her guilt was draining her energy and hugely impacting her ability to deepen her relationships.

Then Julie chimed in, sharing how she's desperate for some girlfriend time, but between work and home responsibilities she feels like she shouldn't take precious free time away from her husband and kids.

Next popped in Jenna, who always felt guilty saying no to requests. She struggled with giving away her time to others, and then felt resentful, overwhelmed, and irritated that she didn't have enough time for herself.

Notice the theme of feeling guilty? When you hear yourself saying, "I feel guilty" or "I feel bad," it's often a red flag that self-worth is a struggle for you. Pay attention, and remind yourself that you, and everyone, is worthy simply because you are worthy. You don't need to earn your worthiness. You were born, as a human being, worthy of love and happiness.

Now, you might be thinking, "Of course I'm worthy. I'm a good person." These amazing women in my group program believed that too. That's the intellectual, rational brain speaking.

But, consider whether you regularly have more thoughts like those above. There's nothing wrong with you if you do! It's just our reactive, old-pattern brain doing the thinking. It's the old stories and interpretations running the show. It's not the naked, clear, clean, and compassionate way of communicating with yourself.

These are your reasons, excuses, or justifications for staying stuck and disconnected. They're totally normal, but not very helpful. Which of these run through your head often?

I feel guilty if …

I don't have enough time to… OR I'm too busy to…

If I were a "good" employee, mother, wife, friend, I'd…

I really should say or do…

Who am I to do this? I'm not that special or important.

Shouldn't I be happy already? I can't ask for more…

For bonus points, go back and fill in the prompts above with thoughts you've actually had. Be honest with yourself about the many ways these thoughts slip in. Start to really experience how these thoughts can infiltrate your day and subtly send signals of unworthiness. Of not deserving. Of not being enough. The endless freakin' hunt for "enough" is exhausting.

Again, it's okay! In fact it's exceedingly common, especially among women, to be a caretaker and somehow place ourselves at the bottom of the to-do list.

However, when you don't feel worthy of having amazing relationships with yourself, your friends, or your partner it has a huge impact on your ability to form the connections that you desire.

So, here's the deeper question that lingers behind a lot of the guilt, the "busy-ness" excuse, and the "shoulds":

Do I really deserve it anyway?

This question can be hard to hear, and it may or may not resonate with you. You may be more in the fear category.

However, most of you will experience it at some point. It might be when things are going really well and there's a new opportunity for you. A big promotion in your career. The love of your life proposes. Your family is booking that Hawaiian vacation. Your husband just told you how beautiful you are.

It might be when everything looks "perfect" to the outside world and you start to wonder if you have it too good. You might worry, "What are others thinking of me?"

As I was writing this book, a former client reached out to me to see if we could work together again. She reads my blog and follows me on social media. She has a sense of what is going on in my life. She said, "It looks like you're living the Rockwellian American Dream."

My gut reaction was to deny how well my life was going because I felt embarrassed and I wanted to be "normal" and fit in. I didn't want to be some idealized version of life. I felt unworthy of this compliment. I wanted to tell her about my fears and messed up self-doubt to prove "I'm just like everyone else!"

In the next breath, I got honest with myself and realized that my life, in many ways, is the "American Dream." Happy, passionate marriage. Work I love. Adorable kids. Not perfect at all, but awesome.

And that's okay. I deserve that.

And so do you.

In my response to her, I laughed and acknowledged that my life is wonderful and I'm happy.

I also acknowledged that I'm human, and just that afternoon I'd wanted to kick my kids out of the car into the rain if they didn't stop yelling at each other.

So, how do you cultivate a greater sense of worth so that you can confidently make connections with the people in your life?

This is a huge question, about which countless books and articles have been written. There's an enormous industry devoted to supporting self-worth and acceptance.

I find it to be a constant area of growth in my life. When I'm faced with my next opportunity or adventure, I have to remind myself that I am deserving. That there is room for more in my life. That there is space for all of us to be happy. That it's okay to love what you have and still want to grow and achieve at the next level. That I am good enough. That I do enough. That I am enough. Enough is enough.

I remind myself constantly, and eventually, it works. I build up a core feeling of worth. I also have many moments of fear, doubt, and guilt. But at my deepest level, I believe I'm deserving of meaningful relationships, fulfilling work, and a happy life.

How do you build your self-worth?

Here are three ways to explore and expand your self-worth, so you can have the relationships you deserve.

1. "Why *not* me?"

I want you to consider yourself in the bigger picture of society, and ask yourself "Why not me?" Think about all the people who are going through their lives around you, who are also striving and struggling to create meaningful lives.

Someone is going to be on *Oprah.*

Someone is going to write the next *New York Times* bestseller.

Someone is going to have a passionate, supportive, and loving marriage.

Someone is going to have a beautiful home with a view.

Someone is going to invent the next lifesaving device.

Someone is going to be the keynote speaker at that awesome conference.

Someone is going to get that job.

Someone is going to take that sweet trip to Europe.

Someone is going to win the Nobel Prize.

Someone is going to start that organization or lead that project.

Someone is going to ask him out.

What makes those "someones" more deserving than you?

Now, obviously, if they've written the book or done the training and you haven't, then they have an advantage. **However, they don't deserve it more. They're not more worthy.**

If there's something you want to create, build, do, have, or be in your lifetime, then you deserve the opportunity to go for it.

I'm also not saying that it all works out if you want it badly enough or work hard enough. I will never win the gold medal for swimming or be the next Adele. That doesn't mean I don't deserve great happiness and success in the areas of my life where I have skills and talents to cultivate.

Knowing that you're worthy of love, happiness, and success isn't about having it all. **It's about believing that you, as a human being, are worthy simply because you are worthy.** I know this can be a tricky one to absorb if you're struggling with your self-worth. But, try to zoom out and look at yourself in the bigger picture of humanity. Try to engage your brain with the idea that worth is not earned. You don't need to prove yourself or be better than others to be worthy of love and happiness.

When you reframe your doubt into the question "Why not me?" it sheds a fresh perspective on an old and tired thought pattern of unworthiness. As I've said throughout this book, because it's so important, you have to shake up the stories you've told yourself. The "truths" are mostly just interpretations. It's time to let them go if they don't serve you.

2. Pure potential, or The baby factor

When my son was born, I was bowled over by the pureness and perfection of this little being in my arms. Most people look at babies with loving feelings, even if they don't want to be parents. Babies show us innocence and purity, untainted by the world.

We all came into this world in this baby form of pure potential. You were born, more or less, a blank slate of possibility.

Very quickly, you begin to have experiences that shape your perception of reality. Your feelings get hurt. You have your first heartbreak. Experience your first failure. You color outside the lines. You mess up on the spelling quiz. You have to have braces. You don't get chosen for a team in gym class. You don't get asked to the prom by the boy or girl you like.

Experiences happen and our stories start to form. We make decisions about what we're capable of and what we're not. Our pure potential starts to become smaller and smaller, until we just see our lives as "the way things are." We settle into the comfortable, so-called reality of our lives. We stop dreaming. Our imaginations get weak. We're boxed into the small "reality" we've accidentally created for ourselves, miles away from the pure potential where we all began.

When you're struggling with doubt, return to the idea of "the baby factor." When you can reconnect with this idea, you have an opening into new ways of seeing things. You have the opportunity to be more courageous, to be more creative, to be whatever it is you're longing to be.

You were born a baby. You were born of pure potential.

I realize that returning to this idea of openness and change is not always an instantaneous phenomenon. However, I've witnessed countless people have extraordinary breakthroughs in how they see the world, and take action, once they've had just a tiny taste of this idea of pure potential.

Part of remembering your own worth is to honor "the baby factor" within you. To realize that you were born with an open path ahead of you, as deserving and worthy as every human being that enters this world. *And you're still as deserving and worthy as you were at birth, no matter what has happened to you or what people may have told you.* Your pure potential is waiting to be revisited.

3. Fact vs. fiction again

Your feelings about self-worth, or lack thereof, likely go back to very early experiences in your life where you decided something about yourself. You probably don't remember it as a "decision" because it felt more like a logical response and you were too young to remember it anyway.

We talked about fact vs. fiction earlier, but it's so valuable in understanding your notion of worthiness that I want to mention it here again.

I can tell you a million times in a million ways that you're worthy, and I truly believe that you are. But unless you can begin to see it for yourself, your ability to have the relationships you crave will suffer. You have to feel that you deserve to be loved, supported, heard, and appreciated in order for others to give that to you in the fullest way possible.

Here's an example of how fact vs. fiction was massively impacting my client Karen, keeping her from having the connections and happiness she so desperately wanted.

Karen would be considered by most outside observers to be physically gorgeous and professionally successful. However, she had always felt like she was the ugly, poor kid who didn't fit in.

When we started working together, Karen's marriage was failing, her hair was falling out, her skin was breaking out, and she felt miserable. Karen knew on some level that she was bright, hard-working, and capable. Yet, she was exhausted, drained, and totally disconnected from her own strengths and talents.

She truly believed that she was a failure because of several messages from her childhood. She'd confused cultural teaching from her parents, who'd immigrated here as young adults, with absolute facts. She'd stopped trusting herself to know what was best for her, because she was always trying to please everyone else and be perfect. She was utterly confused and deeply unhappy.

Karen began to see that her interpretations, leftover from childhood, were crushing her spirit in adulthood. She began to see that they were just interpretations, and that other stories could be made up that would bring her much more happiness. She started to really recognize fact vs. fiction in her own life.

I once said to her, "Karen, you're only 27 years old. You have so much more life to create. So much more you can make happen." To which she replied through tears, "How can you say, *only* 27? I should have done so much more by now."

Here's the thing: she had a very different story about "27 years old" than I did. Her story told her that she should already have children and be staying home to take care of them. My story said that her stage of life was perfect for personal growth, exploration, and career clarity.

Neither story is "fact." I'm not right. She's not right. They're both made up. But her story was breaking her. My story gave her a new possibility and permission to explore.

Consider what stories you're still carrying with you from childhood that are impacting your life today. Lovingly recognize that your youthful interpretations are no longer useful to you. Try creating some interpretations that serve you better, that are more suited to who you are now and who you want to become.

Karen is rocking it. She has a new job where she's a leader in her company. She's dancing again, a passion she'd set aside, which makes her feel beautiful and alive. She's addressing the issues in her marriage with courage, without hiding in fear and shame. She's communicating openly with her parents, releasing them of the blame she'd placed on them from her childhood interpretations. Her old stories creep up and threaten her self-worth, but she now can see them more clearly. She's peeled back the layers and is communicating in a fresh, naked way. And, she's way, way happier.

Chapter 13: What are the costs of fear and self-worth being the boss?

The costs of fear and low self-worth are many and can be catastrophic. When fear and self-worth are controlling your life, there is little room for meaningful connection. Your mind is too busy feeling afraid and questioning your value to find the courage to create awesome relationships. Some call it the lizard brain or your inner gremlin. Whatever you call the nagging thoughts of fear and doubt, they're depleting your courage and costing you big time.

With Karen, she was miserable, and her physical body was literally failing her. She felt completely exhausted and happiness eluded her. Her vitality and relationships were suffering.

I've witnessed many of the losses when fear and self-worth interfere with the courage to connect. I want you to consider if any of these resonate with you. Be honest with yourself. Let yourself feel whatever shows up for you as you read through them. Be compassionate with yourself, with as little judgment as possible, so you can really let in the various consequences of fear and self-worth being in charge.

What are the costs?

A passionless marriage that is boring and unsatisfying.
A heartbreak or divorce.
Living a life without romantic love.
Feeling painfully awkward at every event, meeting, or gathering you attend.
Not having friends you can turn to with your true feelings.
Being exhausted and overwhelmed to the point of total burnout.
Feeling resentment that eats away at your happiness.
Constantly feeling guilty or underappreciated.
Loneliness and a lackluster community.

It has been said that those who are dying regret more what they didn't do than what they did. You can spend your life exhausted and overwhelmed, drowning in a pile of laundry or never-ending to-do lists. The pleasing, saying "yes," putting others first, and guilt can swallow you up, leaving no room for true connection. It is not our mistakes that leave us with regret as much as what we wish we had tried, created, made, shared, done, or said. In this context, consider the costs of fear and self-worth and how they continue to hold you back.

How will you suffer, or how will your life feel unfulfilled, if fear and doubt win?

I know it's not easy to manage your fear or to suddenly feel worthy. But when you can see more clearly what it's costing you, there's a much bigger incentive to disrupt your old patterns, to have courageous conversations, to share yourself more fully, and to be more naked.

If you look at your relationships in all areas of your life, what are the costs for you right now?

Now consider if you continue exactly as you are, what are the costs you can see down the road?

Being vulnerable can be terrifying. Being naked, both literally and figuratively, is scary.

But now you know the costs of not taking the risk, which can help you find the courage to be more naked.

In the next section, I'll go deeply into the transformational, how-to process of naked communication. Some of you have been reading quickly, eagerly waiting for the part that answers, "Yeah, but what do I DO exactly?"

There are definitely clear steps you can take. But if you don't answer the questions above honestly first, they won't be as effective. You need to recognize your old habits before creating new ones. You must strip away communication patterns that aren't working for you, so that you may have space for new ones. Like the old expression, "you need to have some skin in the game," so you can really experience the benefits of going "naked."

I've said that inspiration without action won't get you the results that you want. The opposite is also true. Action without inspiration won't get you very far, either.

Human beings largely exist in inertia, which is defined as "a tendency to do nothing or to remain unchanged." We feel most comfortable with what we know. We often feel scared when we shake things up.

When you deeply know and feel the costs in your life when you allow fear or lack of self-worth to be in control, you are FAR more likely to take *inspired action.* Inspired action will help you achieve the results you want. Inspired action is moving the needle forward based on your true desires.

Part 3: Yeah, But How Do You Actually DO Naked Communication?

By now you have laid the foundation for naked communication. You've stripped down several layers of habits or fixed thinking, and are open to the idea that naked communication can dramatically transform your relationships. At least, I hope that's where you're at! And, if you're still cynical, that's totally okay. But, you might want to think about whether being cynical comes from an old interpretation. If so, is it supporting you in having the relationships you want? Are you scared that you'll try this fresh approach to communication and it'll fail? Or do you want to prove you're right and I'm wrong?

Wherever you're at is completely fine. Resistance often shows up when people are faced with something new and unfamiliar. For example, you're invited to join a really cool creative committee in your community. You know there are interesting people in this group and they do awesome work, but you're nervous. It's new to you, and you find yourself hesitating to say yes to the invitation to participate. You're feeling resistance to the unfamiliar.

Or maybe you're getting stuck because you're like me and like to do everything "perfectly". Perfectionism can also be a form of resistance. People often don't finish projects or share their work with the world because it's not "perfect," which is really another way of resisting being more visible or vulnerable.

When I was doing a lengthy and thorough training with one of my mentors, she always reminded us that we would get the parts we really needed out of it, even if we fell behind or didn't get to all the content. As someone with a story about being an overachiever and perfectionist, this trusting piece was hard for me. Yet, when I could surrender into it and let go of resistance, there was freedom there to enjoy the course, and to trust I was learning and growing at just the right pace for me.

Trust that you are getting value and that something else is possible for you. Practicing clean, clear, and compassionate communication is a lifelong experience. Being more naked in your conversations and connections can bring up fear and doubt. You're here anyway, moving forward, which is extraordinary.

A few years ago I was sitting in a transformational course all about communication. It was day two of the intense weekend training, and we were examining which relationships in our lives weren't working well, where we were holding back, and where we'd simply given up. I'd been studying and practicing personal development work for decades and had done a lot of work on my relationships.

So I was sitting there a bit smugly, not fully engaging with the exercise. But I know better than to think I know it all, so I eventually listened to the nagging voice in my head that kept returning to a colleague I really didn't like. I was resistant as hell. I'd struggled with this relationship for years and had decided it simply wasn't going to change. I'd worked hard to let it not bother me. I did NOT want to have a conversation with her beyond the daily working chitchat. Really, really did not want to do it.

But I did. I used all the naked skills I'm about to share with you, with the foundation I've already laid out. I asked her if she had some time we could talk privately. My heart was pounding and my throat was constricting. I always feel like I'm going to throw up when I'm confronting my shit, dealing with my fear, pushing through my resistance. I could feel what I perceived to be her hesitation, but she agreed to meet.

I was both relieved and horrified. I'd literally allowed my relationship with this woman to cause me countless hours of distress and self-doubt for the past several years. At the time, I wasn't entirely sure why I'd allowed our interactions and conversations to shake me so thoroughly. I can now see that I learned and grew monumentally from that challenging relationship, and I needed that push to get to the next level of my own courage, leadership, and self-worth.

I sat in her office and shared openly and vulnerably about how our relationship impacted me. I asked what I had done that may have upset her. And I listened. I really, really listened while silencing my need to defend myself or be right. Then I took responsibility for what I had said many years prior that had put a rift in our relationship. I was able to see how her interpretation of my words had impacted her, because I used the idea of infinite interpretations.

From that lens, I could really see how I'd made her feel, in her experience. When I could see how my words made her feel judged, threatened, and devalued, I was able to understand our struggles more fully. She wasn't "right" and neither was I. But we were both ready for a change in our dynamic. We each apologized for our part in the ugly and uncomfortable relationship we'd created. We made clear requests of each other about how to move forward.

Before that conversation I had been freakin' miserable with her, and we'd worked in very close proximity, for years. I had totally given up, and resigned myself to "the way things were," until I decided to courageously go "naked" with her. That day I left her office feeling light as air. I was really able to see her goodness and let go of so much anger and resentment. Did we become fast friends? Nope. Did we suddenly love each others' personalities and spend more time together? Nope.

But I felt a thousand times better in her company, as I hope she was in mine. I was more at ease going to work. I could appreciate who she was and what she offered to our organization so much more. I could let go of the exhaustion in the relationship.

It was insanely freeing, and it never would have been possible if I hadn't taken fresh and inspired action. That's the power of naked communication. Years of angst can be lifted, even in the relationships that are a slow and subtle drain on your vitality. Wounds can be healed. You can learn about yourself when you really listen. You can connect anew.

If resistance or resignation are showing up for you, that's cool. Keep reading, trust me that there's power here, and be open to a transformational shift in your relationships.

So far, you've explored several pieces that lay the foundation to break free from your old way of communicating and relating:

You understand that you are always communicating.

You have a sense of how *you* communicate, including areas of strength and areas for growth.

You're willing to embrace the foundational principle of fact vs. fiction, that almost everything is an interpretation or made-up story. That we can choose to make up more empowering interpretations. That if we are willing to see others' interpretations, points of view, and stories, then we are profoundly capable of deepening our relationships.

You're clear that something more is possible for you, your life, and your relationships if you choose to practice this new habit of communication.

However, you might now be thinking, "But how the hell do I actually do it? Break it down for me. How do I get 'naked'?"

So, here's the meat and potatoes. Or the kale and quinoa, if you prefer.

Chapter 14: Naked Communication: Conversation Flow 101

> *"You can make more friends in 2 months by becoming interested in other people than you can in 2 years by trying to get other people interested in you."*
> —Dale Carnegie

Susie and I were walking around the park during one of our regular coaching sessions, talking about how to make new friends. She felt like it was a skill she "should just know how to do." And yet, it made her feel nervous and awkward. She had a story that she'd "always been shy." She desperately wanted to have a group of friends whom she was really at ease with and with whom she could just be herself. But it was scary.

What if they don't like me or aren't interested in what I have to say? What if I share too much and they think my life is a total mess? How do I even begin or get myself into the mix?

These concerns have come up many times with the bright, motivated, and dynamic women in my life and work, and some men too.

So I started to break it down into steps you can actually practice. Since we've already established that we're yearning for meaningful and fulfilling relationships, and that is what has you reading this book, let's dive into how to have conversations that are more likely to foster true connection.

1. Be in flow.
Conversations should go back and forth. If you think about a casual game of catch or a leisurely tennis match (not Venus-vs.-Serena style), there's a relaxed exchange between those playing.

Conversations that build connected relationships, not just sustain surface-level rapport, have a give and take. Questions and answers. Sharing of experiences. A dance between the people involved, where everyone gets a turn on the stage.

Put simply, you shouldn't do all the talking or all the listening.

Many women have told me that they feel like others talk at them for minutes on end about stuff they're not even interested in hearing. Or that some people feel like "energy vampires," always sucking up all the air and positive energy when they spend time with them.

This is not the way a loving and meaningful relationship should feel.

Ask yourself if you have relationships that feel imbalanced in this way. Now, consider what you can do to bring it back into *flow*.

If you're the one doing all the talking, stop yourself and return to your commitment to actual connection. Ask the other person a question. Ask for their feedback. Or whether they've ever had a similar experience to the one you're talking about. Simply be quiet and allow them to offer something to the conversation.

I've had to really train myself to be better at slowing down and listening more. You've probably already realized I love people and have a lot to say! My brain moves quickly and I'm eager to share. But, if I want to have flow in my conversations so everyone feels heard and valued, so we can build deeper connections, I've got to shut up sometimes. My husband and best friends lovingly remind me of this!

If you're doing all the listening, notice if this is a pattern in your relationships and ask yourself how you can speak up more clearly and share yourself more boldly. Politely interrupt and offer an idea or an insight. Question why you hesitate, whether it's an old story running the show or fear creeping in. Dig in to your courage and go for it. Remember that you're worthy, and therefore your thoughts, feelings, and contributions have value in an authentic relationship.

The lovely, bright, and "shy" Susie and I would practice together. Building up her courage required some preparation so she didn't feel like a deer in the headlights in social situations. She came up with several stories about her life that were funny or interesting, so she had an arsenal of things she could offer up at a moment's notice. We practiced with me over-talking and her finding a way to "butt in." We wove in some helpful life raft phrases, so she didn't feel scared of awkward lulls in conversation. A year later, after courageously putting herself out there and reaching out to people, she'd successfully made it through several social situations that had previously been terrifying for her. From her commitment to build relationships and share herself more openly, she'd created an amazing group of friends.

Once you've gotten more comfortable with conversational flow, you might find a need for boundary setting with some people. You'll start to recognize more easily when you have a pattern with someone that isn't in flow and be able to communicate your need for change.

For example, if you know that one of your friends, family members, colleagues, or whoever always talks your ear off, let them know at the beginning of the conversation how much time you actually have to listen. When you start doing this, people will begin to value your time differently. They won't assume you have endless time to listen to them ramble on. This isn't unloving or rude. It's simply returning the conversation to flow, and strengthening the opportunity for deeper connection by valuing your own time and worth along with theirs.

I've answered my phone and said, "I'd love to talk to you, and I only have 10 minutes right now." I really want to be present and available when I'm in conversations with people, so I try to set it up to be successful. I've had friends say the same to me (because I know I can be a talker!). I so appreciate it because it helps me simplify what I want to share with them in the time we have together.

Setting up boundaries is respectful, and sets up the expectation that both people are valuable in the relationship. When you're clear, you feel much less resentment and frustration from imbalanced relationships. You set the expectation of flow, exchange, and sharing. The so-called energy suckers either don't stick around because you no longer endlessly give them your time and attention, or they adjust and learn to have more give and take in the conversations, thus creating more opportunity for true connection.

2. Be curious.
People love to feel seen, heard, and appreciated. They want others to find them interesting. They want to talk about what interests them. Even those who are shy really appreciate when people want to learn more about them and get to know them better (and actually, many shy people appreciate this approach even more than others because they find it harder to keep up a conversation that is focused on other people).

I had a client who was in the dating world. She's smart, successful, beautiful, creative, and generally awesome. She had no trouble getting dates, but she was really looking for a partner. She wanted a man who was up to interesting things in life, would support her in her own growth and success, and was fun and loving.

But so many men fell short of her desires. We identified that they weren't bad, but they weren't *curious.* They didn't ask enough questions about her interests, passions, work, etc.

Showing curiosity, which usually means asking questions, demonstrates interest. It shows the other person that you want to connect. That you want to learn more about them. That you're willing to invest some of your time in hearing about their life.

Curiosity is hugely helpful on the path to greater connection. When a conversation stalls, ask a question. When you know you want to make a new friend with the energetic and lively mom at student drop-off, ask her a question about herself. When you want to learn more about the person you're on a date with, ask him a question about his life. When your marriage feels flat, get curious and ask yourself what you could do to bring in more passion.

Use open-ended questions to get the richest answers, such as, "What was that like? How did it go? Why did you enjoy it so much?"

Questions that can be answered by a simple "yes" or "no" don't usually add more energy to the conversation or move it into greater depth. Open-ended questions, in comparison, are an invitation for intimacy. You're being truly curious and giving the other person a chance to share more about themselves.

3. Push pause on judgment.

Human beings are judging machines. We size people up the second they walk into the room. What they're wearing, how they talk, where they went to school, what they do for work, how their kids are behaving. It's an automatic response.

I think it's bullshit to say we're not judgmental. I also don't think it makes you a bad person. But it can screw up your ability to form deep and loving relationships if you don't bring awareness to it.

Here's how to deal with our human "judginess" as it relates to naked communication.

Practice "pushing pause" on those judgments long enough to actually aim for connection. Recognize your judgments for what they are, simply your opinions, and don't believe them as truths. They're your interpretations of what you're seeing and hearing. They're subjective.

In order to make more meaningful connections and strengthen our relationships, we have to suspend our overly active judging minds long enough to listen to a person. Long enough to see if they make us laugh, if they're doing interesting work in the world, if they enjoy the same music that we do.

When we automatically categorize others with our judgments, we deprive ourselves of the opportunity for connection.

I was so very guilty of this when my older child started elementary school. We got to choose which public school he attended in our district, and we agonized over this choice. Ultimately, we selected the "hippie-artsy-earthy" school, and I was freaking out a bit.

Our dear friend had been a teacher there for 15 years, and her daughter attended the school. She encouraged us to check it out and not let our judgment get in the way until we'd seen for ourselves what the school was really about.

I was already at war with myself for considering a school that wasn't our neighborhood school. "All the schools are excellent. We're so spoiled by having more choice. Why are we even visiting the other schools? How elitist can we get! My husband teaches at the local high school; we *should* just do the normal path."

We visited. We loved it. We decided it would be amazing for our son.

I went to some of the pre-kindergarten gatherings in the

park, so my son could meet other kids and feel more comfortable before the school year started.

Immediately, my judging mind went crazy. "Oh my gosh, none of the moms work. I can't relate. No one lets their kids watch TV. They think Disney is the devil. They grow all their own organic food and make their own soap. They loathe makeup. They'll think I'm too intense. They're so closed off to the real world, living in their privileged bubble. I don't fit in. My kid won't fit in. This was a bad idea. What the hell were we thinking?"

You get the idea. It was ugly. My judgment was in overdrive, and not in a good way.

From this place of judging, there was NO space to connect with anyone in this new community. I was literally severing myself from an entire group of parents because I had decided we weren't a match. I was putting myself on an island where it was me vs. those weirdos.

I feel so embarrassed to admit what a judgmental bitch I was being in my head, but I've already told you we're automatic judging machines and I'm no better.

Except, I work to catch myself in my judgments as quickly as possible and return to my commitment to naked communication, to authentic connection. I've learned a lot about communication, connection, and relationships.

Mostly, that I LOVE people and that relationships are the heart of happiness, fulfillment, and success.

So, I pushed pause on judgment. I got out of my own way and I started talking to some of the moms at the park meetups, and later at pickup and drop off times at school.

I've met amazingly bright, creative, and lovely women. They're writers, lawyers, teachers, and yes, some are stay-at-home moms. Most have televisions and a few don't. They eat healthily, raise chickens, and are often makeup-free.

We're all moms and women who are doing our best to raise little humans while maintaining our own passions and identities. We talk and laugh. We connect. I drop the F-bomb and talk about my work. They tell me about essential oils or a new project they're working on. We share stories of the trials and tribulations of getting the kids out the door in the mornings. It's lovely, and I now look forward to seeing them and getting to know them even better. I have a whole new community that wasn't possible when I was stuck in judgment.

I would have missed out on so many new friendships and connections if I'd let my judgments rule the day. I could have stayed separate, looked for "evidence" that they were different from me. But, how lonely is that? **It's way more fun to connect.**

4. *Be you.*

I saved this one for last, because it's at the heart of all connection and it can feel really challenging. Being yourself is a courageous act—perhaps the most courageous act there is in this whole connection business.

Start by considering how often (or not) you feel like you're allowing yourself to be fully *you* in your daily conversations.

Here's how you can assess this you-ness more:

Are you thinking about what you're going to say next while the other person is still talking?

Do you play the conversation over again in your head afterward, worrying that you offended someone or didn't say the "right" thing?

Do you leave the conversation mad at yourself because you didn't speak up about how you were really feeling?

Do you laugh and find pleasure in talking with certain people more often than not?

How do you feel when you think about going to a gathering where you don't know people well but you know you want to connect with them?

When you answer these questions honestly for yourself, you can begin to see how much or little you struggle with being yourself in relationship to others. You might notice that you hold back from sharing your jokes, your quirks, your secret Star Trek obsession. You might realize that there are some places in your life where you show up more effortlessly, and others where you're totally suppressing your true self.

Now, be compassionate with yourself here. Don't go into judgment overdrive with questions like, "Why the hell do I do that? Why don't I just act like myself?" It's totally normal to want to look good in front of others and to want to fit in.

Sometimes it's scary to offer more of your true self to others. But it's also totally exhausting to try to be somebody you're not. When you're constantly playing it safe, holding yourself back, being cool, it zaps your energy. It also makes it hard for people to connect with you because they don't really know YOU.

Nobody wants to tell their struggles to a perfect person. When you aim to be yourself, your most real and raw human self, it gives others permission to do so also.

When you strive to be in flow, be curious, push pause on judgment, and be more of yourself, you will experience huge shifts in your conversations. You'll find it easier to relate to others. You'll feel more comfortable and natural when you're interacting with people. You'll be more open to forming deep connections.

Chapter 15: Naked Communication: The gift of "getting it"

Don't you love it when someone totally gets what you're trying to say?

Or when they fully understand how you're feeling or where you're coming from?

Every one of us wants to feel seen, heard, and understood. It's a core longing that we all share. When you can master giving this gift to someone else, you can resolve conflicts with expertise and ease, as well as strengthen any connection that you have with others.

One morning I was sitting in my office at the middle school where I worked, when a parent came in to speak with me. She felt the school was not treating her child fairly. She felt that nobody understood her kid. She wanted blood. She was furious. She felt wronged and hurt and she was very, very angry.

Earlier in my career, this situation would have scared the crap out of me. I wouldn't have felt confident how to respond to such overt rage and frustration. However, I quickly learned to use a skill my parents had taught me, and that I'd studied further throughout my life and work. It's a skill, and also a generous act, to simply "get" the other person's experience in that moment, no matter how uncomfortable it may be or how much you might disagree with their point of view.

"Getting it" begins with the open-slate listening we talked about earlier. It requires being present, and not distracted by the thoughts your head. In this situation, it wouldn't have been helpful to be caught up in thoughts like, "She's crazy. What the hell am I going to do? I can't handle this."

Getting it also requires letting go of being right, like we previously discussed. In this moment of her fury, it was completely irrelevant whether or not her son had been wronged or the school had actually failed him. What *was* relevant was that she felt someone was listening to her and willing to hear her point of view, her interpretation, her "truth."

I knew this mom's child well. He was a tough kid. Many of his teachers were very frustrated by him and no longer knew how to support him. Some had simply given up on him. I knew this mom well. She'd been in my office several times before and she could get hot mad. I looked at her and said, "I totally hear how frustrated and mad you are. I really get that you want what's best for your kid. I'm so sorry that it's been this hard."

In that moment she began to settle down. I invited her to discuss how, together, we could better support her child. She relaxed, began crying instead of screaming, and together we made a plan to help him as best we could.

We never would've gotten the outcome that we did had I not really "gotten her" first. She needed me to really understand her point of view, her feelings, her deep emotional response, and her fears. She needed to know that I thought her concerns were valid. It doesn't mean they were the "truth," but they were her reality and I had to communicate that I got that in order for us to move forward.

"Getting it" is the most profound gift you can give to your relationships and to others because when someone gets you, it feels extraordinary.

Think of the global implications if people slowed down and tuned in deeply to other people's experiences before jumping in with solutions, opinions, and strategies. It's the profound gift of listening *and* expressing that you've truly heard someone. There would be so much more mutual respect, so much more possibility of connection, so much more hope for resolving conflicts.

Getting it doesn't mean that you fully understand their experience. It means that you let them know that you understand that their experience is their experience, and thus it matters.

For example, I went to both high school and college with a gorgeous, bright, passionate African American woman. When the news was awash in horror stories of senseless deaths of black men and retaliation toward law enforcement, she wrote a gripping piece on Facebook. I was deeply moved by what she wrote, but I struggled with how, as a white woman, to respond.

Then I told myself, I cannot begin to "put myself in her shoes" because I am not a woman of color living in this country at this time. However, I can simply "get" her by acknowledging that I read her piece and that the struggle she shared was powerful to me. I could do my best to have her feel seen, heard, and understood.

In my decade as a school counselor I cultivated this skill of "getting it" that allowed me to defuse almost any conflict that presented itself. No matter how angry or irate a parent was, I could calm them down and come to a reasonable resolution of the situation. This is the almost magical result of "getting it." Think about how this skill could support your relationships, from your partner to your colleagues to your kids.

It's truly transformational. It literally allows us to strip away all that is between us and the person we're speaking with, and dig into the nakedness and honest truth of each other's' experiences. Remember, vulnerability is scary *and* we all just want to be seen, heard, and understood. You can use "getting it" in your most intimate relationships or with total strangers.

Have you ever been at the store and seen a mom (or dad) with young kids crying, fussing, and screaming, and she looks like she's at her wits' end? You can offer the gift of "getting it" by turning to her and simply saying, "I remember those days. It's so hard sometimes." In that moment she feels seen, but with compassion. She feels like her life right now is understood. Maybe she's less embarrassed or lonely as a result. It's a beautiful opportunity for naked connection.

I strive to use this tool with my children as much as possible, but of course I screw up too. It takes a conscious awareness, a slowing down, to really tune in and "get" someone. You have to exercise the muscle regularly until it becomes a new habit.

For example, my seven-year-old son was crying and angry because our plans had changed. We were no longer doing what he thought we would be doing for the day, and he was pissed. Part of my brain wanted to say, "Get over it. Be flexible. You have such a good life, can't you just appreciate it?"

I knew that response would not resolve the distress he was feeling and would actually escalate his frustration. It would also weaken our connection instead of strengthen it. Instead I said, "I totally get how disappointed you are, buddy."

Now, did he snap right out of it? Of course not. He's seven years old and still learning how to regulate his range of emotions. But I was showing him that I understood where he was coming from. I was demonstrating that I was hearing him. I was supporting our relationship by "getting it" in that moment.

Once you or someone else feels like they've been heard, seen, and understood, without defensiveness or righteousness, *then* you can discuss possible solutions. When you're in a conversation with someone, and you're truly getting each other, there is an almost magical opportunity to build a stronger relationship. When you feel understood you also feel valued. It's a powerful foundation from which to deepen the connection.

Chapter 16: Naked Communication: What happens when you don't "get it"?

Oh, it gets really, really messy. Dirty, instead of clean. Muddled, instead of clear. Righteous, instead of compassionate. Yet, this is how conversations often go. It's no wonder connections falter and creating depth can feel impossible.

We often talk at each other while distracted by our own thoughts. We're thinking of what we can say next to offer a solution or support. Or we're thinking of our counter argument or justifications. Of how we can prove our point and all the evidence we have to show that we're in fact "right." Or maybe we're thinking of all the other things we need to get done and wishing the conversation would end already.

We forget to pause, tune in, and actually be with the other person long enough to "get it." Literally, this can sometimes take just 10 seconds. If you're really present, and you're thinking about naked communication with connection as your goal, you can often see, hear, or feel what the other person needs you to "get" very quickly.

When you don't get what the other person is trying to communicate, or someone doesn't get you, there are two likely responses that will occur:

The person will try to force their point. They will continue to talk and talk and talk with various arguments and perspectives until they feel like you have actually gotten them. They may go on and on, and become increasingly frustrated by the fact that you don't seem to understand them. This pattern will screw up any relationship over time.

The person completely shuts down. They feel like you don't get them, you don't understand them, and perhaps that you're not even listening. They stop talking and stop trying to share themselves with you. In that moment the opportunity for connection is lost. They've decided that you don't understand who they are or value them enough to truly pay attention. Or that you're rigid and unwilling to consider their point of view. This pattern will also take you down to lonely town real quick.

Consider which of these two reactions you have when you feel like someone just isn't getting you. You've likely fallen into both categories at some point in your relationships, and it's helpful to think about it so that you can understand the gift of "getting it" even more.

A common thing that trips people up with "getting it" is the desire to be helpful or fix a problem. In our eagerness to make the pain or discomfort of the other person go away, sometimes we jump right into solutions, ideas, or suggestions. While there's nothing wrong with wanting to help, support, or serve, it often isn't received well until the person feels they've been heard.

Another common pitfall is the automatic response to defend, justify, or explain. This reaction comes up often in conversations when you feel threatened, blamed, or accused in some way. If you can notice your reaction, take a moment to pause, and then remind yourself that "getting it" isn't about agreeing with the other person, you'll do much better at maintaining connections in those hard conversations.

It's about really letting them know that you listened to them and understood their point of view. It's the great bomb diffuser and the great intimacy ignitor.

Chapter 17: Naked Communication: Come from LOVE

My mom has taught me many things, but this one is at the top of the list for helping me be a better leader, wife, mother, and friend.

"When you come from love, you can say *anything*. When you don't, you can say *nothing*."

I had a client whose marriage was rocky, to put it lightly. How the story went (because, remember, these are all just interpretations and stories) is this:

They had grown apart. He wasn't on the same path she was on. He hadn't fulfilled his end of the bargain when they'd gotten married and wasn't who she thought he was. There was animosity, resentment, and frustration galore. There was a major loss of love and affinity.

So, you can imagine, when he tried to give her any feedback at all, she wasn't having it. It could be a suggestion about dinner, and she'd dismiss it as selfish. It could be an insight about her behavior, and she'd be enraged at his hurtful commentary.

It didn't matter what he said—he literally could have said she looked lovely in her new outfit, and she'd likely have thought he was being manipulative. He could say nothing to her that she would hear.

You can see that this is problematic. In fact, it's catastrophic if it's your marriage and you've severed all ability to communicate with your partner because there's no love left in the foundation of your relationship.

Now, have you ever had someone in your life, a best friend, a coach, a teacher, a boss, whom you just knew adored you? They loved you and respected you. You felt appreciated by them and safe with them.

When those people give you feedback, even when it's constructive in nature, you listen. You listen because you know they love you and want what's best for you. You trust that they have good intentions. They could say almost anything to you, and you'd be willing to consider their input.

With this client, we were working on simplifying her life in order to find the confidence, clarity, and happiness she so desperately desired. We were exploring how she could trust herself more and pursue what she deserved. I noticed a pattern with her, as she kept responding to her challenges with an "all or nothing" approach.

We've all done this. "If I quit my job and go to Bali for three months I'll finally feel free and relaxed." Instead of asking ourselves, "How can I feel free and relaxed more often now, in this life I'm already living?"

When I pointed out that the "all or nothing" mentality was holding her back from what she desired right now, she laughed. She said her husband had often told her that she does this "extreme choice type of thing."

But, she never listened to him. She'd dismiss his input as judging, hurtful, and spiteful because she didn't feel he was coming from love. Which isn't necessarily true, but it's how she was experiencing him.

When I made the suggestion that she slow her roll and reflect on simplifying, seeking freedom and peace in her current life, she was totally on board. In fact, she was thrilled about the idea, and we immediately put it into action by using her vacation time for short, fun, mid-week adventures.

She heard me because she feels loved and respected by me.

This is a hugely important component of the work I do. I have to establish a rapport with the people I work with so they know I adore them and am 100% on their team. Without this foundation of love, I can't effectively ask challenging questions or give honest insight into their growth and desired results.

Here's a simpler example. You're getting dressed to go to a wedding. You're not sure which dress looks better. Both your sister and your friend are there, and you ask for their opinions.

Your sister tells you that the red dress looks better. But, because you've often felt like she's highly critical of your appearance and has called you fat in the past, you dismiss her suggestion. You're not sure she's coming from love.

Your friend then says she also thinks the red dress looks better. You immediately decide to wear the red one because you know your friend adores you and would never want you to go to the event looking anything but awesome. You're sure she's coming from love.

When there isn't a foundation of love (or you can think of it as trust and respect), it's very hard to communicate effectively how you feel, what you want, or how to solve a problem. In fact, it can be nearly impossible.

So when you need to give feedback or have a difficult conversation, you can come from love by reminding yourself that your commitment to the relationship is bigger than your need to be right, bigger than your fear, bigger than wanting to look good. There is no "how" to do this, other than wanting awesome relationships more than you want anything else. Go back to the earlier things we discussed— think about what you like about the person, think about all the interpretations that are possible in this situation. Commit to love. Commit to the relationship. And then speak from there.

I know sometimes you're not feeling the love for the person you need to talk to. You're angry or hurt, so you're wondering, "How the hell do I come from love in those moments?" I'll talk about how to use naked communication in your more challenging relationships later in the book. For now, think about the history and soul of the relationship, where the love once lived, and try to be present to that when you're in a conversation with that person. Or, if you really can't find a way to come from love, maybe it's not the time to give the feedback or share the suggestion. The more you can participate in any relationship with a loving mindset, the easier it'll be to build depth and connection.

Chapter 18: Naked Communication: Be willing to be "wrong"

Remember the foundational idea that there are a million interpretations to any situation? This is essential for happiness in your relationships, particularly in conversations where there's a history of conflict or an anticipation of conflict.

If you work from the paradigm that your "truth" is just a story, you can really listen to and be with the person in a fresh and open way. This is HUGE.

But you've got to let go of being right. Instead, remind yourself that connection is your goal. You don't have to prove anything. You're worthy because you're worthy. Besides, being right is sometimes just a fleeting happiness, with a big, long-term cost.

As humans, we are hardwired to be right, which can also look like proving others wrong. We want it almost as much as we want food and air and water. Ugly as it may sound, it feels so damn good to think "I told you so." We don't even realize how much this desire runs our lives.

I was recently out for a night with some newer friends. Someone brought up politics, and it became clear that one of the guys in the group didn't share the same views as the rest of us. I could feel my inner need to be right mounting, and to "prove my point," thus making him wrong. And, I had the support of everyone else in the group, so it would have been so easy to dig my heels into being right.

Ten years ago I would have launched into a tirade about how right my perspective was and, subsequently, how absolutely wrong he was. Instead, I took a deep breath and got curious. Here was a highly educated, kind man who I knew to be a loving father and husband. We were all in a social situation, getting to know each other better. If I got on my high horse to be right, I would miss out on the chance to connect with him further and perhaps learn something new from his point of view.

We had an interesting conversation about our differing political views and a really fun night. Did I still think I was right? Yes. Did I still express my own views? I definitely did, but I didn't put those beliefs above my desire to connect. I had my opinions and he had his. We listened and learned and laughed. My need to be right didn't kill a new friendship before it even had a chance to start.

Proving we're right can be so insidious, and wiggle its way into our lives in ways that can devastate our relationships and our happiness. Mostly, we don't realize we're doing it.

When we can let go of this need, and be okay with other perspectives, stories, and interpretations, it's a game changer.

It's a foundational principle to mastering effective naked communication that gets you the fulfillment you desire. It also may be one of the hardest, because being right feels oh so good.

I used to listen to a beautiful folk song by Kreg Viesselman, who sings with a huge heart, "We talk and talk until we're full. The more I push, the more you pull. You pull so hard you fall right out the door. And I sit befuddled, all by myself. Drain the bottles on the shelf, and I wonder what I started pushing for."

In our most intimate relationships, like our parents or partners, we can get so hooked by the need to be right. It feels like a more personal slight and we get more triggered. For example, I told my husband about an upcoming social event that I'd added to our calendar. I was absolutely sure I'd discussed it with him. I usually handle the calendar for our household, and I'm pretty good about keeping us all up to speed.

The day of the event rolled around, and he was clueless that it was happening. He swore I never talked to him about it. I swore I did. I *knew* I did. I was right, damn it. Why didn't he pay attention to the calendar? Why didn't he listen to me? It could have gotten really ugly really quickly.

But, in reality, did it matter? If I checked in with myself, what I really wanted was to go to the event together and have a good time. Who cares if we miscommunicated over the calendar! We could work on being clearer next time. We'd never know if I did or didn't talk to him about it because that fact lies in our memories, both of us believing we were right. We were fighting about something that could never be proven either way and, in the meantime, was eroding our relationship.

If you can take a moment to pause and ask yourself "Is it worth it?" you'll be surprised how often your answer is "No, it's not."

Can you think of at least one argument that you've had where you were fighting so hard to be right and afterward you realized how silly the argument was in the first place? Think about it.

I've caught myself in this loop a million times, because I'm human and I love to be right.

Like, "Why the hell did I just spend 15 minutes arguing with my husband about who helps out more around the house?" We both help a ton. Let's just appreciate each other more, which is what we really want more than being right.

Notice how often this inclination to be right shows up for you. Try to pause before you launch into your argument to prove yourself, and instead consider what you really want to get out of the conversation. What would help strengthen your relationship? What would bring you closer to that person? You can still state your opinion. You can still make requests for change. But you don't have to do it with an intense attachment to being right that positions you in a battle stance with the other person.

Always ask yourself, do I want to be right, or do I want to be happy?

Chapter 19: Naked Communication: The power of the ASK

Building the relationships and the life you want involves action, as you know. Wishing, waiting, and hoping aren't nearly as effective as clean, clear, and naked requests.

How are *you* doing at asking for what you want and need?

I was 23 years old and out to change the world. I'd graduated, with honors, and headed to Kenya to teach—a dream I'd had since childhood. When I got back to Philly, I landed my first "real" job. I was working in four inner-city middle schools under a federal grant. I was fired-up, idealistic, and invincible. Until I felt the pea-sized lump above my collarbone. After the surreal experience of a biopsy and several doctor appointments, I learned I had Hodgkin's lymphoma, a cancer that would require chemotherapy and radiation.

When I heard the doctor give me my diagnosis, I dropped the phone on the floor. My dad was sitting next to me on my couch in my cool, twenty-something-style apartment in Center City. I remember the exposed brick wall and fireplace, the stairs up to my roommate's loft bedroom. It was all there, waiting to be enjoyed, when the phone fell from my hand.

That moment flipped the script on my life and impacted the way I approach life forever.

I learned a million lessons from that challenge in my life. **Perhaps the biggest was the reminder that life isn't a guarantee and so I wanted it to be freakin' awesome.** I wanted to create a life of love, excitement, and impact. There was a sense of urgency about living that I didn't have before, and this urgency has encouraged me to keep creating those desires in my life again and again, no matter the fears or doubts.

I learned that in order to create the life I wanted, I'd better figure out what I really wanted and how to effectively ask for it. I better really go for it. I'd always been more outspoken than most. I'd always been adventurous. And I'd always wanted a big and impactful life (thank you, Mom and Dad, for modeling this type of lifestyle for me!).

But now, there was a sense of urgency around that lifestyle that drove me. And I have a feeling that you may have some of that urgency too, which is why you're reading this book. You're tired of freaking waiting for life to turn out. You're a soul searcher, who's always learning and growing into the next level of your greatness.

After I was given a clean bill of health, I decided to follow my best friend and move to Colorado. Excitement, remember? I thought it'd just be for a year. Fifteen years and a couple of kids later, here I am. The gorgeous outdoors, calmer pace of life, and amazing community stole my heart and smoothed some of my intense edges. It allowed my spirit to heal after the earthshaking experience of cancer and survivorship. There was room here, space for my own expansion, and loads of sunshine.

I got a master's degree in counseling psychology and worked in the public schools for a decade. During my time as a school counselor I learned a ton about conflict resolution, communication strategies, relationship dynamics, empowerment, self-confidence, and more. I grew personally and professionally in my time as a counselor. Schools are the trenches of a growing society, where young people are courageously navigating the tumultuous journey of becoming themselves.

For a while, it was the excitement and impact that I craved.

And then I had my second child. I sat on my couch on maternity leave, dreading my return to work. Not because I didn't want to work; I really did (I'd be a terrible full time mom. I know my strengths and weaknesses!) But because I was ready for the next adventure. A bigger way to use my passions, skills, and creativity. A fresh way to impact the world. Which is what led me to you. To writing this book. To coaching and speaking.

But to make this enormous career leap, I had to courageously ASK for what I wanted.

I had a very stable career with a pension plan. I worked nine months of the year, which was the same schedule as my teacher husband. I got to help teens and families, be a part of a team, and effect change in my community.

It was a pretty big ask of my husband for me to leave the job security and go out on my own. He's a teacher, remember? We needed two incomes for the life we loved to live. He's also a pragmatist. He's incredibly supportive, but this was uncomfortable for him. And it was scary for both of us.

How did I get him on board? I used naked communication to make the ask. We talked about it a lot, from our fears to our yearnings. We were as clear, clean, and honest as we could be. Eventually we found our way onto the same page by using our naked communication skills to connect, listen, share fully, and co-create our future together with this change. These same skills have helped us through our conflicts, our parenting challenges, the death of my dad, 5,000-mile family road trips with our kids, and keeping the passion alive in our marriage for over a decade.

Since starting my business, I've had numerous opportunities to practice asking. It's part of the hustle of creating your dream. Making connections. Making requests. Communicating powerfully. Building intimacy. Getting what you want. Having your needs met.

I'm going to take you through the exact process of how to ask for what you want using the principles of naked communication.

However, it'll be way more powerful if you actually read this section with a real-life example from your own experience at the forefront of your mind.

I want you to pause and think of something that you want in your life right now that you don't have. Or something that you'd like to improve or augment.

Now, winning the lottery, losing 50 pounds, or becoming the next Taylor Swift aren't going to be the most useful examples for this activity.

You want to choose an area of your life that is happening right now and that is real for you.

Keep these specific desires in mind as you read through this part of the book. As I've mentioned repeatedly, inspiration alone will not get you the results you desire. Taking action is the key piece to causing meaningful change and getting the relationships and outcomes you're craving.

(Remember, the exercises and resources are all included in the book guide to help you move forward at www.sagebhobbs.com/bookguide.)

The ASK Formula

There are four key steps that will help you ask for what you want in a way that will most likely get you what you want. They're way more simple than you might think, but it doesn't mean they're always easy. We have a way of complicating things, based on our fears and self-worth patterns. We can get triggered, freaked out, or worried, especially when courageously asking for something that is important to us.

In actuality, these four steps are profoundly simple and effective. So, place your stories aside and be open-minded when you read the ASK Formula. Give yourself the opportunity to try something new, something that could completely transform how you live your life and build your relationships.

1. Know what you want.

This topic alone could be a book, because knowing what you want can feel daunting at times. For some of you, this question will stump you. It may have been a long time since you actually paused to consider what you really want. Many people are busy going about their daily lives, completing tasks on the endless to-do list, and going through their routines. Stopping to reflect on whether or not your routine is still aligned with what you want isn't something you're often taught to do.

You may have become disconnected to your own longing or resigned to "how things are." You may be the most big-hearted, generous giver and you've become so used to taking care of others you lost yourself along the way. Or you may be too scared to admit what you really want, for fear of upsetting people. Perhaps guilt stops you from owning what you actually want.

This first step is essential because no one else can know what YOU really want.

It seems so obvious. Yet, as you grow up, your life fills with relationships, stories from your past, disappointments, responsibilities, and on and on. In that whirlwind of adult life, you rarely pause long enough to truly consider what you really want.

You may feel happy, and if that's you, awesome! It's still important to ask yourself this question regularly so YOU are consciously checking in with yourself. Is this still what I want? Does this relationship still excite me? Does this work still interest me?

Because it's really hard to get what you want if you're not clear first.

You want to be awake and driving the car, aware of the road you're on, making the turns you want to make to have the life you want to live.

Take a moment to consider what you want for the different relationships in your life. Be as specific and honest as possible. This is an exercise *for you*. Try not to let old stuff cloud it or muck it up. Go with the first thoughts that come to mind, before your patterns have a chance to pounce and shut down your desires.

- Your love life
- Your friendships
- Your colleagues
- Your children
- Your parents
- Your siblings

To dig deeper into these, ask yourself, "And what else do I want? And what else do I want? And what else do I want?" The more you ask this question of yourself, the more you will uncover about your deeper desires.

It may feel uncomfortable at first if you're not used to truly considering your own needs and wants. It's funny, because I watch my young children all the time very clearly ask, and even demand, what they want. Kids feel they have the right to ask for what they want. They feel deserving and worthy. From their perspective, it sounds like, "Of course I should ask for what I want! Why wouldn't I? And I should get it too."

However, this habit gets worked out of you as you grow up. You're told not to be selfish. Generosity and humility are celebrated widely. Sometimes you get so disconnected from knowing what you want that you really struggle to identify what makes you happy.

Who says you can't be an incredibly generous, thoughtful, and humble person who is also clear about your own desires and courageous enough to ask for what you want and need?

If you're finding this activity difficult, keep going. Truly all of the elements of naked communication that I've shared come together beautifully with practice, persistence, and patience. As your relationships begin to deepen, your ease with building connections grows stronger, and your requests are met more frequently with "yes," you'll see that it's more than worth the effort.

For right now, think of the specific examples you came up with at the beginning of the section. Ask yourself what you want in relation to those specific examples.

I'll give you an example from my own work. A client of mine had her second child. She had taken time off from her career to be with her kids. Her employer had given her time to decide whether or not she wanted to return to work. It was approaching the decision hour. She was stressing out enormously about what she wanted to do.

She felt anxious about leaving her children with a childcare provider. She felt anxious about not maintaining her career, some financial independence, and professional identity. She felt guilty about "wasting" her graduate education by staying home. She was really struggling with how to move forward and make this decision at this junction in her life.

We worked through a similar exercise as I've listed above, digging into what it was she really wanted. We had to peel back some of her feelings of guilt, old messages of "shoulds," and loosen the intense feeling of responsibility that was burdening her. Ultimately, she said, "I really just want to work one day a week." In her next breath, she said, "but I know that's just totally crazy and I could never ask for that."

I asked her, "Why not?" The old adage of "It never hurts to ask" came to mind. We discussed the possibilities of making such a request of her boss. We worked through several scenarios, and all of the doubts and fears that went along with those scenarios.

She was scared of feeling embarrassed by making this unusual and bold request. She was scared her boss would say no. She was also a bit scared that her boss would say yes and she would feel guilty for getting exactly what she really wanted. There was a lot to work through in order for her to have the courage to make the request.

However, once she was clear that working one day a week was truly what she wanted, we were able to work out a strategy that included a lot of courage for her to make the request and ask directly.

The result: she works one day a week and is loving it!

2. Make a *clear* request.

Once you have done some of the internal work that helps you be clear about what you really want, then it's time to actually make a specific and clear request.

For many people this can be much trickier than it seems. Again, fear and self-doubt may rise up to obstruct your courage. In naked communication, clarity is essential to having the best chance at the desired outcome.

Implying, hinting, and hoping simply aren't as effective, although they're what many of us do by default. It's a lot less scary to hope, hint, and imply than to directly ask. You risk nothing by simply crossing your fingers and hoping for the perfect marriage, the dream job, the ideal schedule, the best romantic getaway, the peace to be restored in your family. There's nothing wrong with hoping, wishing, and dreaming, but they're not naked, honest, and courageous acts.

Clear requests are beautifully naked. They don't have any manipulation with them. They respect the other person because they don't require any guessing. They're an opportunity for engagement that is fully transparent. They're so refreshing.

For example, I wanted to speak at an event in Denver. I'd applied but hadn't heard back yet. I emailed the organizer and said, "This is my topic. I'll rock it. If it doesn't work, that's totally fine. But my bold request is can you book me in for this month's event?"

I was very clear that I was asking to be a speaker at that particular event. I didn't write to the organizer in an implying, murky way such as, "Just wondering about the status of my application. The upcoming topic looks really interesting to me."

See the difference?

The organizer replied promptly and enthusiastically offered me the opportunity to speak. I know it doesn't *always* work out as we hope, and I'll talk about that more in step four, but when we don't make a clear request it almost never works out at all.

Another example, which I know many of you may relate to, is desperately wanting something from our husbands or partners.

My husband is truly amazing. He's loving, supportive, encouraging, and helpful. He's passionate about his work, our marriage, and our kids. But I want him to be "romantic."

He thinks he is. I disagree. There's no right or wrong in this situation, as it's really an issue of differing interpretations, like most things!

I could make a case for why my idea of romantic is better, and battle with him about it. Early on in our relationship that's what I did, looking for evidence to prove he wasn't romantic and that I was right about it. The result of that approach? He wasn't any more romantic, so I didn't get what I wanted. He felt underappreciated, which caused less love and affinity in our relationship. Totally ineffective strategy.

Another angle could be to hint at what I wanted, by mentioning that Dana's husband brings her flowers all the time or sweeps her away for surprise getaways. I could cross my fingers and hope that one day he'll get the hint and I'll find myself surrounded by candlelight and flower petals.

But, the hinting, hoping, and implying won't really get me the outcome I desire, which is to feel more romance in our partnership.

I've had to go more naked, and share my true desires more honestly with him. I've had to get vulnerable and tell him why I need to feel loved and honored by "romantic" acts. Initially, it wasn't easy for me to do because I felt embarrassed that I, a strong and confident modern woman, even wanted romance. I had self-worth issues around it, such as, "Shouldn't I be happy enough with how *almost* perfect our relationship is? I shouldn't want more."

Once I opened up more honestly with him, it was abundantly clear that he wanted to make me happy, and that I have to make clear requests so that can be possible. Instead of my old strategies for improving romance, I tried, "Can you buy me flowers sometimes when I don't expect it? Or leave me a love note occasionally? Or kiss me when I'm washing dishes?" These requests, which were clear examples of what romance means to me, were easy for him to say yes to. I got what I wanted, and, ultimately, he did too.

Now it's your turn. Really think about where have you been implying, hinting, or hoping.

I know if can feel scary and vulnerable to be more direct, but it's way more powerful and effective. And, you're not going for average relationships, you're going for beautiful and meaningful ones.

So, where can you courageously make a clear request instead?

3. Appreciate and acknowledge.

This is the BEST-kept secret to successfully getting what you want. It's my super power tool, and it can be yours as well.

First, you have to be willing to consider that you could improve in this area. Many people dismiss this idea because they think, "I'm polite. I say thank you. The people I love know I love them."

However, I've found that most people have a lot of room for improvement when it comes to mastering appreciation and acknowledgment in their lives. It requires a degree of vulnerability, courage, and open-heartedness that can make you uncomfortable. But you've gotten this far, and I know you're ready to rock this piece! Appreciation is possibly my favorite thing to do in both my personal life and professional world. When you offer it as honestly, and nakedly, as possible it is one of the most heart-filling experiences. Add in truthful acknowledgment, and you have a powerful recipe for asking for what you want.

Here's how appreciation and acknowledgement work.

Appreciation

Appreciation can have many definitions. Within naked communication, appreciation is the profound, specific, and authentic gratitude shared with someone else for the way they make a contribution to your life. It is far beyond a simple thank you, though that is a good start. Appreciation is a powerful tool in leadership and in everyday connections.

For example, I had a favorite boss in my previous career as a school counselor. She was my favorite boss for many reasons, however, a significant skill of hers was the art of appreciation.

I can remember leaving many contentious and heated meetings with families or with fellow colleagues, and having her pull me aside for 30 seconds to offer some appreciation of how I'd handled the situation. She would thank me for my ability to defuse upset parents. She would thank me for listening to the two very distraught teenagers with compassion and understanding. She would thank me for handling a training, where there had been some pushback, in a way that people felt heard.

She offered specific appreciation for my unique contributions and skill sets. This went a long way in my desire to support her work, to make her job as leader of our organization easier, and to perform at a higher level because I knew I was valued.

When you can *clearly and specifically* thank people for what they bring to your life, your team, or your home it can deeply strengthen your relationships. Literally, naked appreciation can completely transform your relationships—even the hard ones that you may have given up on.

When the time comes to make a request, and to build the connected and meaningful relationships that you desire, appreciation is the heart of it. Remember, you and everyone else wants to feel like you matter, like you uniquely provide value, like you're seen and loved.

In your personal relationships, appreciation is a profound way to foster greater depth and intimacy. It's a very naked way of showing how much you truly value and love someone. I like to pour on appreciation thick, like gravy, sometimes making people slightly uncomfortable even as they soak it in and a smile spreads across their face.

Acknowledgment

Acknowledgment can have more than one meaning, but for the sake of this discussion acknowledgment is to recognize what your request might mean for the other person. You want to acknowledge what the impact might be. It demonstrates that you're thinking beyond yourself and your needs and you're respecting that the other person is involved in the request.

For example, my husband likes to play in a basketball league. Every year when the season is about to start, he asks me if he can participate. There's an impact that evenings away has on our household rhythm, with our children, and on me. He acknowledges that impact when he's making his request.

It sounds like, "I know it means you'll have to manage the kids and dinner without me. I know sometimes you're worn out by then and that's the crazy time with the kids."

Right away he's made me feel understood and acknowledges how his request could impact my life. I feel like he gets it and is honoring my experience. I'm more likely to say yes.

So, how do you use appreciation and acknowledgment to ask more effectively for what you want?

The sandwich approach.

The sandwich approach is a simple structure for making a request. You appreciate someone specifically and authentically. You then make your clear request. And you end it with the acknowledgment of what this request's impact might be on the other person. The key is to be absolutely sincere, clear, and full of appreciation.

A strategy that is commonly used for leaders to offer feedback to their team members is to provide one thing they're doing well, then an area for growth, and lastly another thing they're doing well.

It's similar with the sandwich approach I lay out here. When you surround a request with sincere appreciation and acknowledgment, you really honor the other person and give them permission to truly say yes or no. It's pure, naked communication at its best because there are no hidden motives, it's honest, and clear.

The sandwich approach is so simple, but of course that doesn't mean it's easy. You'll likely need to think it out in advance when you initially use it. With practice you'll begin to integrate it into the natural flow of your conversations and life.

Here's an example. When I first started my business I wanted to invest in a million different programs and trainings. I *love* to learn and to be masterful with things I'm passionate about. I had "shiny object syndrome" when it came to an amazing book, conference, or learning opportunity. I was drawn to those shiny objects like a wild-eyed two-year-old in a candy store.

My husband knows this about me, and mostly he loves my passion and enthusiasm. However, he is great about chiming in with a dose of pragmatism and thoughtfulness. So, when I wanted to hire a coach at a significant investment point because I knew it would help me uplevel my business, I used the sandwich approach to make my request.

The quick version went like this, "Babe, I so appreciate the million ways that you support me and my passion. You have been unwavering in your belief in my work. You've helped out so much with the kids so that I could take the time I needed to grow this dream. Thank you so much. (appreciation) I'm ready to grow my business in a bigger way and I really think hiring this coach will help me reach my goals. Can we make it happen? (request)I know it's an investment and that you would rather I put the money in our savings or for that sweet vacation we've been talking about. I know I've been guilty of chasing shiny objects in the past and that has been frustrating to you at times. (acknowledgement)"

The sandwich approach is an effective *and* respectful way to make requests. Yes, I could have just spent the money. In our partnership it wasn't about "permission," but about agreement and mutual decision making so that we both feel valued. It's a super powerful way to ask for what you want and need in all areas of your life.

4. Be with the response: yes, no, or maybe

This is hard, but it's incredibly powerful. When you can accept any response to your requests, you feel free to make more requests.

People who are successful in business make a lot of requests. They play full out, and they don't stop going for it when they get a no. I've also seen this in the world of dating, when the desired outcome is a long-term commitment. People who are willing to go on a lot of dates, regardless of the outcomes, have better odds of finding a partner.

Not only is nonattachment powerful for you, it also helps you get the results you desire. Other people feel free to give an honest answer when they can feel that you'll be okay with their response, even if it's a "no." They will feel your confidence, and you will train your brain and body to be more comfortable asking. It's a win-win.

Again, I'm not saying that being unattached to the outcome is easy. I'm pretty sure Buddhists have spent millennia discussing and striving for the art of non-attachment. It can feel painful to get a "no." You might feel rejected, hurt, or slighted. It's okay to feel however you feel! Let those feelings come and go however you need to, knowing they are feelings (not facts) and they will pass. Then, get back to the commitment of becoming "naked." If you want to be wildly successful in getting what you want, you have to be willing to deal with the sting of some "nos."

Successful, powerful people, with lives that are working for them, make a lot of requests. For example, my mom transitioned from being a family therapist to a vice president of a transformational consulting company in her forties. She had no background in business but was well-versed in making requests and getting things done. She became extraordinarily good at sales by making thousands of calls to ask for business and being really okay with any outcome. She had to be okay with the "nos" so she could get back on the phone and keep making the calls. And because she gave potential customers the space to truly say yes, no, or maybe, she was able to engage many of them in more discussion and eventually close more deals. She kept asking, regardless of the answers.

Now it's time for you to put it all together. There's a worksheet for you to practice in the free book guide at www.sagebhobbs.com/bookguide.

Go back to your original example from your own life when we started this section of the book. Choose one person and one request you want to make. Keep it naked, as specific and clear as possible. Use the sandwich approach to appreciate-request-acknowledge. Give them the true freedom to actually choose yes, no, or maybe. Experiment, explore, try it out again and again until asking becomes integrated into your new, naked communication DNA.

Chapter 20: Naked Communication: Who are you hanging out with?

I hung up the phone and exhaled a sigh of relief as a smile took over my face. I then returned to my computer and got back to work, back on track and ready to go after a quick detour to self-doubt and fear central.

I'd been writing an article, designing a course, and planning a Women's Circle. I had several projects going at that time, and I'd found myself spiraling into WTF land.

As in, WTF am I doing? Is any of this going to work? Is it worth it? Do I deserve to have it even better? Ultimately, the underlying gremlin, do I have what it takes? (Remember that whole fear thing?)

So I called one of my trusted fear-slayers, aka my friend Katie. Katie quickly and lovingly got me out of the BS stories in my head and reminded me of my value and gifts (Remember that whole worth thing?). Katie has been my friend for well over a decade and is a constant cheerleader and supporter in my life.

One of the sweetest parts of our friendship is our unwavering belief in how awesome the other person is. We're not blowing smoke; we truly see each other as bigger and greater than we can sometimes see ourselves.

In my coach training program we talked about the idea "The environment always wins." It's been similarly said that "You're a result of the people you spend the most time with." This theory was also explored when I was studying counseling psychology and family systems—that those in our lives help shape who we are.

This essentially means that those around us have a profound influence on our lives. When I worked as a school counselor for a decade, I saw this often among my students. Those who hung out with kids who got into trouble had a hard time keeping themselves out of trouble, even if they were well-meaning kids. Those who hung out with high achievers usually strived to do better themselves.

Building a community who supports you wholeheartedly is essential to your sense of connection, happiness, and fulfillment. You're now a naked communicator, and you'll be more likely to stay that way and grow into it even more, if you have others in your life on a similar journey.

Do you have some friends who just exhaust you or who always agree with you about how hard life is? You may feel guilty admitting it, but when you hang out with them you feel drained. You might have a long history together and love them deeply. But, you're not your best self when you're together.

Do you have other people in your life who are up to exciting things? Who have happy marriages or interesting work? They usually approach life with a lens of optimism, even when things are shitty. When you're with them, you feel like maybe something more is possible for you and your life. You have a taste of their enthusiasm and it feels good. They share themselves honestly, imperfections and all, making you feel more at ease with your own humanness.

This section can be a bit unsettling for people, because you might be thinking, "Sage, what am I supposed to do? Divorce my family? Ditch my friends?"

My answer is yes and no.

First, take a moment to reflect on the people you spend your time with. Actually pause and write a list. This list includes people in person, on the phone, on Facebook, and so on. Write down your colleagues, your kids, your friends. Really think about your day from start to finish and who you spend the most time talking to.

Second, ask yourself how you feel when you're connecting with each of them. Do you feel loved and appreciated? Do you feel inspired and hopeful? Do you feel drained and worn out? Do you feel irritated and depressed?

Be very truthful in this process. No one will see this except you. It's in exercise for you to examine your community and begin to determine if it's the community that works best for you in your happiness and fulfillment. You're being curious about your environment and whether or not you're supported, loved, and connected in a way that helps you thrive.

As you do this, do your best to suspend judgment of yourself and them. There's no right or wrong in who they are as people. Remember, our feelings about them are just interpretations anyway, not absolute truths.

Last, let's return to the idea that "The environment always wins."

You want to have more loving and meaningful relationships, or you wouldn't still be reading this book. You want to have greater happiness and fulfillment in your life, and you now know that deeper connections are the key.

So, as you've figured out what you really want and how to get it, the next clear step is to create a community that supports you in achieving this outcome.

Simply put, find your support crew. Look for opportunities to cultivate connections with people who inspire you. Spend more time with the people who also want to grow and evolve. Make an effort to consciously build a community that you love and with whom you feel genuinely connected.

In the process, it's okay to gently let some relationships go.

A while back I was out to dinner with my graduate school friends. We live in different areas and only get together a couple of times a year. We all studied to be counselors, so we go deep quickly and talk like crazy to catch up with each other's lives.

Mary asked for our advice on "breaking up" with a friend of hers. As counselors, we'd all been trained in communication and resolving problems, but this was tricky. As we talked, it became abundantly clear that this friend was exhausting Mary. She also wasn't adding any real value to Mary's life. They'd mostly become friends out of convenience, because they lived in the same neighborhood. With great relief, Mary decided to let the relationship go. When we all got together again recently, she mentioned how freeing that choice had been.

Please don't mistake this exercise as ditching friends when they're down, or scrapping everyone and starting over. I've had friends going through hard times with family illness, marital struggles, or bouts of depression. I still love and support them, of course. Because who they really are at their core, are amazingly bright, generous, and fun people who love and support me.

If you do this activity and you begin to notice that you're the caretaker of everyone in your life and it's exhausting, you want to consider a change in your environment. If you realize that you really don't have the level of depth and intimacy that you crave with the people you spend time with, you'll want to nourish your connections so that you do. Or if you feel judged for your growth and transformation, you'll want to make some new friendships that think your evolving self is amazing and fabulous.

We can't choose our family of origin, but we can choose our partners and friends. Why not choose ones who support you in being awesome? Who make you feel good? Who cheer you on?

If the old standbys of fear and worth are coming up for you, that's perfectly fine. It takes time to forge new patterns, and to not allow our old reactions to govern our lives. Naked communication is about pattern disruption, so you can begin again with a fresh approach in every conversation, every opportunity for connection.

It takes courage to make new friends or share more honestly with old ones. Just like being physically naked, being emotionally naked is a bold and beautiful act.

But, you now have the awareness and tools to make it happen. You have the heart and desire to build the relationships you want. You are a naked warrior on the adventure of a lifetime.

Chapter 21: Naked Communication: When the shit hits the fan

Many people come to me when they're struggling with their relationships. Sometimes it's a relationship with someone else. Other times it's the internal struggle in their relationship with themselves. Either way, the path to healing is the same: digging deeply into being naked. Getting real about what you want, what you deserve, how you can ask for it, slaying fear, finding courage, sharing your heart, and huge doses of compassion.

I don't sugar-coat the challenges of life. I've had my own hardships and the profound honor of supporting countless individuals through their own. When you shake up the status quo and strive for greatness, you'll come up against some shit. You'll recognize which relationships in your life are the hardest for you. You may want to run from them or stay comfortably in your own safety zone of old patterns.

For some of you, those relationships will be your mother or father. For others, your husband or partner. Or perhaps your boss or your sister. Or your kids. Kids can push every button you have.

For me, it's my kids. I have amazing relationships with my kids, but they're also the relationships I'm most intensely attached to. I want them to be the best of the best. I want to be my best self for my son and daughter. But, there are times when all of my knowledge, practice, and skills as a communication expert fly completely out the window and I find words coming out of my mouth in a volume and tone that do not build depth and connection, to say the least.

I screw up. You'll screw up. They'll screw up. Remember, everyone's doing the best they can with the skills they have.

When shit gets hard, return to the beginning. Remind yourself of your worth. Remind yourself of your power. Remind yourself of how to use naked communication. Be clean, clear, and compassionate. Practice, practice, practice. Let go of what isn't working, both old stories and relationships that don't fulfill you.

And remember, when you are playing full out, conversations don't always go as planned. As I mentioned before, relationships can be crazy messy. Relationships include people's feelings, interpretations, and old stories. Sometimes you say something that you regret, or that gets misunderstood. Sometimes you say something and it comes out with more anger or hostility than you intended. Sometimes something you say doesn't land as you'd hoped, and you find yourself in a disagreement or straight up fight. This is how it goes.

However, when you return to your naked communication framework, you know how to clean things up quickly and restore the love. Cleaning things up is what I call handling conflicts effectively and beautifully, with repairing the connection as a primary goal. You take responsibility for the part that was yours. You authentically apologize for however you contributed to the conflict. You make a clear request of how to move forward in a way that works for both of you and nurtures your connection. These are the essential steps of cleaning up a disagreement or misunderstanding.

The other day I had an argument with my husband. I felt frustrated that when he was responsible for the kids on his own, he seemed exhausted and like he couldn't deal with them. I was working and on a phone call in a different part of the house. I could hear them yelling at each other and running around the house. At one point, my daughter came flying through the room where I was working.

When I had a break I came downstairs to check in. I found myself, obnoxiously, picking on my husband. I said accusingly, "Why is it so hard for you to be with the kids on your own? I was just trying to do some work. You took them to the movies. It should've been fun. Why are they running around screaming at each other?" He simply replied "okay," again and again with each admonition.

I got increasingly irritated. (As I told you earlier, we have different conflict styles that we always work through, but still make us stumble. We both strive for naked communication at all times, and we still have to catch ourselves and recommit.) In a not-so-great indoor voice, I said, "Why do you ignore me when you know I'm upset?"

He said, "We just handle things differently. I thought the kids' conflict was totally normal and that they were working it out on their own. I'm sorry I let her get away from me while I was building with him and she ran into your room. That was my fault. But I feel like I was handling them. It was under control. Sometimes they're just hard and get under my skin, but I've got it covered."

The lightbulb went on for me: we needed to clean this up. We were fighting over different points of view, neither of which was actually "right." We were totally wasting a summer afternoon and putting a dent in our relationship if we continued to stay stuck and "right."

We were supposed to all go on a family walk. Instead of telling him to stay home and take some time to himself, which is what I had suggested when I was caught up in being right, I realized it would be much more fun for everyone if he and I figured things out and reconnected.

I took responsibility for my part by acknowledging that I can be inpatient, which is my biggest communication challenge. I lose my temper more quickly than I would like. I apologized for snapping at him, without even listening to him and his point of view. I requested that he take the kids out of the house, or keep them quiet, in the future when I'm working. I also requested that we all go on the walk and have a good time. I told him I loved him, and off we went.

Because this was a small disagreement, the cleaning-up process was easier. We weren't dealing with massive betrayal or years of pent-up resentment. However, it's the small disagreements that can erode and destroy a marriage or friendship if they're not resolved well. I've seen it with women in my life and my work—that the vulnerability and courage needed to clean up disagreements feels so scary that they simply don't do it. Or the need to be right keeps them rigidly stuck and spinning their wheels. They let the disagreements "slide." And the resentment, hurt, and disconnection build up.

When you know in your gut that there's been a rift in one of your relationships, you've got to clean it up. You might be the one to initiate this more often than others, because it's hard and many people avoid the messiness of restoring love and connection. But it's always, always worth it. When you clean things up, your energy isn't drained by holding on to old wounds and you maintain more affinity in your relationships.

Cleaning up is a forever practice. Always and forever in relationships we will have to clean things up. I promise it gets easier and more natural the more you do it, like all of the naked communication practices. And the rewards are the relationships you desire, but dang, sometimes you won't want to do it. Do it anyway.

And when it's so hard you can't see the forest through the trees, forgive. The ultimate act of naked surrender is to forgive so you can be free. I'll talk more about forgiveness in the next chapter. It's something I'm constantly working on, and will be forever, because it always helps *and* it can be damn hard.

Unfortunately, not everyone will meet you in the middle as you reach out to deepen your relationships. Some people are so uncomfortable with being vulnerable that it's almost painful for them. Others are really stuck in fear or doubting their worth. Often people are just so used to the level of depth that they've always known and they don't realize something else is possible for them. They simply haven't been exposed to the skills or ideas that would give them the path to greater connection.

In these cases, you'll have to be the "leader." You'll have to really go for it with your naked skills, knowing that you can't change them but also remembering that you don't want to box them in with your judgments of them. Let there be room for them to surprise you! With as much compassion and courage as you can conjure, start opening up to them with the intent to connect more deeply. Try asking deeper questions and wait for their answers with clear listening. Or share a bit more personally about your life. Maybe ask for their advice or guidance where you wouldn't usually.

Be prepared that you may or may not get the response you desire. If you feel disappointed, I totally get it. Here's what I have to say about the risk of trying naked communication with those who aren't super responsive: First of all, it's about YOU. You want to be a loving, open, real, and courageous communicator. You want to embody that naked self as often as possible because the more you do, the more natural it will become and the more connected you'll be in the world, even if not with this particular person.

Second, keep trying. Some long-standing relationships, where the people have deep individual and relational patterns, may take a longer time to make inroads. But if you continue to be a stand for your own amazing and courageous "nakedness," you will likely see some growth in this relationship over time.

Last, remember that section about building your community? When you have many deep and meaningful relationships in your life, there isn't as much urgency or desperation that they *all* be that way. You get your needs for deep connection met by some people in your life, and it takes the pressure off those other relationships where you're still working to cultivate the depth.

For example, your dad may have a hard time showing his love and affection openly. He might not fully understand your passions and interests. He might not give you the guidance or reassurance that you crave when you go to him for support. But, if you know you can get that love and reassurance elsewhere, that you can get filled up by your partner or best friend, then you have more space for your relationship with your dad to be whatever it is without the pressure and judgment. You should still keep communicating nakedly and aiming to deepen the rapport, but you won't feel nearly as attached to the outcome if your community is full of other strong and loving relationships.

Chapter 22: Naked Communication: Forgiveness

> *"Courageous people do not fear forgiving*
> *for the sake of peace."*
> —Nelson Mandela

Forgiveness is one of the single most powerful things you can do in your life, hands down. It can also be one of the hardest. Especially when you feel deeply hurt, betrayed, or wronged by someone. It can feel impossible to give up being right about what the other person did. You can get incredibly stuck in this pattern of hurt, blame, and anger.

Forgiveness is NOT about absolving the other person of wrongdoing. You're not letting them off the hook. You're not dismissing their actions or behaviors.

Forgiveness is for YOU. It's for your freedom. Your happiness. Your desire to have amazing relationships. Your ability to share yourself authentically.

Being angry or hurt is actually totally exhausting.

Ultimately it's a choice. You can choose to forgive because your commitment to your own happiness, to building meaningful connections, and to greater fulfillment is BIGGER than your hurt or anger.

Sometimes it's little things and sometimes it's big things. All are equally important. What makes a big pile of crap? A lot of little slights, hurts, arguments piled on top of each other. Forgiveness in the everyday is hugely important to the quality of your connections. It's one of the most powerful tools you can use to transform yourself and your relationships.

About halfway through one of those epic 5,000-mile road trips with my family, my son really pissed me off. I was standing outside of the car, about to run into a store to grab something quickly, and we were talking through his open window. When he didn't like something I said he rolled up his window in my face, with a bit of an eye roll to match.

In one of my not-so-great parenting moments, I put my head through the other window and called him a rude spoiled brat. Then I went into the store.

This could be considered a small incident. Many people would just let it slide. Some would say that I was justified in my response.

However, I'm committed to awesome relationships so I knew I couldn't ignore what had just happened. In this situation, I also happened to be the adult who wants to teach my child how to forgive, take responsibility, and resolve conflict.

I took some deep breaths while walking the aisles of the store.

First, I had to forgive myself. Whenever one of my kids acts out, I'm faced with my recurring fear that I'm a shitty parent who's raising an entitled brat. Since raising amazing humans is the most monumental task I've ever taken on, and it swallows my whole heart because I SO want to do it well, it's really scary when I feel like I'm failing at it. My rational brain knows this isn't true and that I'm doing the best I can, and mostly a damn good job. I also know my kids are deeply loved and cared for, and that they have two parents who strive to teach them about life in a meaningful way.

So, I had to forgive myself for the ways in which I may be screwing up as a parent by being human. I had to forgive myself for losing my temper and resorting to name-calling. I had to forgive myself for being someone who gets impatient more quickly and more often than I'd like to admit.

Then I had to forgive him for being rude. This felt easier than forgiving myself. He's seven years old. He gets upset when he doesn't get his way, like every kid I've ever met. I know he loves me and he's doing the best he can.

I went back to the car and said, "I'm sorry I lost my cool, buddy. I'm really sorry I called you a brat. It made me mad when you rolled the window up on me, but I'm sorry for saying that to you."

To which he replied with a very sweet apology as well. But, even if he hadn't, I had already done my forgiveness work. I was forgiving myself and him regardless of his response, and I already felt a million times better.

Forgiveness offered. Relationship restored.

A friend of mine has been in the throes of a sad and painful divorce. They have a beautiful child together, and like most of us, started out their journey together full of love and hope for their future. However, the struggles mounted over time to a point that was soul sucking. They worked hard, with both professional and personal support, for years. They tried, they cried, and ultimately it was time to let it go.

In this case, forgiveness has been more elusive. It's been hard for my huge-hearted, generous, and insightful friend to find forgiveness. His actions caused her a lot of suffering. She's felt heartbreak and anger in waves so big she's felt as if she's drowning.

Yet, she seeks to forgive. In some moments she feels this grace, and she can exhale and feel the load of disappointment and rage lift from her shoulders. In others, she slips back into that space of feeling sorrow and anger so cutting as to take her breath away. And then again, her commitment to happiness and freedom brings her back to forgiveness.

In the darkest hours of your relationships, you may have to make this choice to forgive again and again. And again. It's really a lifelong practice.

However, when you choose to make it a part of your life, you'll find that you can do it more quickly and easily over time. You'll feel the benefits of forgiveness so clearly, that you'll be more eager to do it, knowing that you can feel lighter, freer, and happier. Forgiveness is for *you*. When you're not carrying around anger, resentment, or painful disappointment you're much more able to give and receive love and connection.

Chapter 23: Naked Communication: A WARNING

Sharing vs. over-sharing for your own benefit

Sometimes when you unlock the floodgates of communication for people who've been holding back, playing it safe, or keeping their opinions politely buttoned up, it can be like a firehose has been aimed at all of their friends and family.

A firehose is not the art of naked communication for deepening connection. A firehose drenches you before you have a moment to come up for air. It feels like ambush instead of the beautiful ebb and flow of a naked conversation.

As I shared with you earlier, when my husband and I first got together we quickly realized we had different communication styles. This played out in various ways, from how we handled conflict to how we expressed our affection.

Mostly, I talk more than he does.

In some ways, this works beautifully for both of us. I offer appreciation constantly, which makes him feel loved and valued. I bring up areas of disappointment or frustration so we can work it out and restore affinity and connection. I encourage him to call his mom or reach out to his brother, because I'm a stand for his relationships and happiness.

In other ways, he's had to teach me the beauty of subtlety and letting go. He'll say, "Sage, not *everything* needs to be said."

At first, I thought he was crazy and just plain wrong. I grew up in a family that honored communication as a core value. I trained as a counselor and a coach. I work in women's empowerment, and support people in finding (and using) their voice. Not say *everything*? Nonsense.

I quickly realized how beautiful this idea is to deepening connection, if used prudently.

Kitchen cabinets left open doesn't have to be a big discussion. When you've had your feelings hurt, you talk to the other person about that incident, with the goal to resolve it and reconnect. But you don't go on and on about the million ways that you've been hurt throughout your life. Remember, naked conversation is an exchange. You don't want it to be all about you, leaving others exhausted after talking to you. You don't have to overwhelm people with your feelings or desires. You don't need to bare your soul to an innocent stranger on the plane who happened to get seated next to you.

The danger of over-sharing is different from the idea, "If you don't have anything nice to say don't say anything at all," which can be suppressive.

You don't want to hold back or harbor resentment within your relationships. That never works.

Naked communication is about using your words mindfully, so you don't over share all over someone and leave them feeling exhausted, used up, and ready to run away from you as quickly as possible. The goal is connection, not simply to relieve yourself of pent-up emotion.

You want to remember to listen when you're connecting. You want to share what's most important to share, but not necessarily everything. You don't want to deliver a monologue. You want to engage in a balanced way, and with connection as the main goal. Remember the "flow" of conversation that I talked about in Chapter 14? It's a dance, a rhythm, that has space for all involved.

A few months ago I was at a women's business lunch and was asking these bright and passionate women about their struggles with communication. This idea of being "unloaded on" came up more than once. Many women expressed feeling that others take advantage of their kindness, or their generosity, by talking their ears off.

The experience of unloading, or being unloaded upon, completely screws up the opportunity for connection. If you pay attention to your conversations, you'll notice which role you play more often. If you are the unloader, practice really assessing what it is you most want to say that will strengthen the relationship, not just make you feel better. If you often feel unloaded on, practice your own boundary setting. Let people know you only have a few minutes to talk. Politely interrupt and excuse yourself. Once you set those boundaries, people will usually know them and feel them. You won't be the one they "corner" anymore to deliver their monologue.

Ultimately, sharing is meant to bring us closer to others, not just to hear ourselves talk.

Chapter 24: Naked Communication: Practice to make the naked you real

Remember that piece about "inspiration without action won't get you the results you want?" As you finish this book and go about your life, you'll keep some of the *ah*as that really stuck for you, and others may start to fade. Transformation is a lifelong game. The more you practice, the more the layers you shed will actually stay off. The more you engage with naked communication, the more natural it will feel to form and maintain the deep and meaningful relationships that you adore.

As with anything, practice brings mastery.
You can practice making connections anywhere with anyone at any time.

Every year my family takes its annual trip "down the shore." I share my nostalgic memories with my children, and watch as they enjoy the experiences I did as a kid: funnel cakes, hours of digging in the sand, sloppy pizza, ice cream, seagulls, and boardwalk rides.

This year we pulled into our usual parking lot to find it full. I decided to ask a man who was working in the parking lot where else we could easily park. Because I was friendly and connected with him by saying, "Oh we come down here every summer from Colorado. We always park here because it's so perfect. We're not sure where else to park, any suggestions?" he responded with friendliness. He said, "Well, you can park over in a different lot a few blocks away, but you can also check out the lot here to see if there's a spot still open that I didn't see."

He moved the cones aside and we decided to take a gamble by looking for a spot. We made it a game going up and down the rows, asking the parking gods for a spot. BAM, in the last row, one perfect spot was waiting for us. When we went to pay the nice man he was so surprised and happy that we'd found a spot.

As we were walking out of the lot toward the boardwalk, my husband mentioned that we found that spot because we had bothered to stop and talk to the man who was working there and he allowed us to check for one last spot in his lot. Moments like these are small but awesome.

Everyday conversations, when using naked communication, can create a more pleasant experience and great outcomes, in this case the perfect parking spot. They also make you feel more connected to your neighborhood, community, and those around you. Talking to cab drivers, to the other moms at the school bus drop-off, to your waiter, to the checkout people at your local grocery store, or to your neighbor is an incredible way to feel like you're a part of the bigger world in a meaningful way.

Life is more fun in connection.

While cultivating deep connections is the goal of going naked with your communication, you can practice this skill throughout your life in a million small, fleeting, human connections. It's so powerful to go through life able to generate connections anywhere you go, from a party to a networking event to your bedroom.

A few hours later on our boardwalk adventure, I found myself with another opportunity to create connection. I placed my daughter on the hopping frog ride, strapped her in tightly, and went back out of the gate to watch her have fun. I said to the young man who was working the ride, "Not a bad summer job looking out at the ocean and helping kids have fun and feel happy." He offered me a huge smile and replied, "Yep, it's a pretty good deal."

I watch the world around me all the time, an obsessive observer of human interaction. I love people and I love how I feel when I'm connecting with them. I'm always curious about how I'm coming across in conversations and how others are relating with each other. Most of the parents who were taking their kids on the boardwalk rides said nothing to all the young people who were working around them. There were hundreds of us humans sharing the friendly, family amusement park space. It took less than one minute for me to chat with the young man working the frog ride, and I felt a surge of happiness at our shared connection.

Sometimes my son tells me I'm embarrassing. Embarrassing your children is not a new phenomenon. However, occasionally he is referring to my friendly behavior connecting with strangers. I've decided it's more important for him to see connection in action, so he learns the benefits of cultivating relationships, than it is to worry about his embarrassment. I'm sure that if I didn't embarrass him in this way I would embarrass him in another way, regardless!

Even though he's embarrassed, he also often smiles to himself about it. On some level, I think he thinks it's cool. Recently I was driving him and a friend in our car (the car is an incredible place to be quiet and listen to your kids' conversations without butting in). He and his buddy were chatting about the different kids in their class and reflecting on first grade. They were talking about who got in trouble often, the challenges of playing with certain kids during recess, and other moments about their social world.

My son then says, "The new kid said I was his first real friend at school and it was really cool. It was awesome." I remember when the new student joined their classroom mid-year and my son mentioned that he'd tried to talk with him a bit. Of course I was proud of him for being kind and inclusive. But, when I heard him talking to his friend in the backseat, I realized how happy it made him that he had forged this meaningful connection with the new boy in class. They hadn't become best friends, but my son had reached out for connection instead of taking the safer path to stay with the familiar.

We adults can learn a lot from kids. They're often much more able to be naked (clear, clean, and compassionate) when they talk to others. They simply haven't built up as many stories that increase their fears about being vulnerable.

I don't even think about having these kinds of conversations with people in my daily life. It's just part of the practice of who I am. I've probably always been more outgoing and extroverted than some people. We all have different personalities and communication styles that come naturally to us, which makes our efforts to connect both beautiful and messy.

You want to practice at *your* own edge. You want to play with fresh opportunities to make connections with new people you encounter, as well as within the relationships that you already have created in your life. It's not about doing it *as much* as someone else. It's about practicing naked communication enough to build the relationships *you* desire.

You want to look for opportunities to pursue that are slightly outside of your comfort zone, a little more vulnerable and naked than you're used to. As you practice, keep in mind that the biggest commitment is to build connections and nurture relationships. When you keep that commitment front and center it helps you find your courage in the process.

If you could see inside of my life you would see that it's not perfect. (And if you know me or read my blog, you know this already!) It's damn good, and passionate and full of love, but not perfect. Relationships can be messy. Especially when you're committed to them being extraordinary, beyond the status quo. There will be disagreements. Conflicts happen. And, hopefully, resolution happens also. It's really important to recognize that this isn't about blame or shame, wrong or right. It's really about *being* in relationship with others.

Chapter 25: Naked Communication: So how do you put this all together?

> *"Dig deep and go for the light."*
> —Danielle LaPorte

You start by returning to what you want first. You have to know in your heart what your vision is of the life you want to create. You don't have to know every detail. But you have to believe that there's the possibility for the deeper connections and relationships that you crave in your life. It's the reason you picked up this book in the first place. It's what had you start to read it and continue to read it. If you've made it this far in the book, there is something that you want from your relationships that you are willing to go for. There is something that you crave and that you yearn for in your connections with others. If you can keep that yearning present when you are in conversations with your friends, family, colleagues, or even strangers you'll be much more likely to use the naked approach and be more clean, clear, and compassionate. You'll be more open and vulnerable, with greater opportunity to connect, when you stay true to the desire you really have for connection in your life.

You return to pure potential. Pure potential is magic. It's when you're clear about all that is possible for you and your life. This is my favorite step. It's also one that trips people up. Your potential is that baby-like state that we talked about earlier. It doesn't mean immaturity. It doesn't mean denial. It doesn't mean naïveté. It's the pureness that we're all born with. The tabula rasa, or blank slate. Your pure potential is still inside of you. Your ability to create a life you really love by returning to that sense of open possibility is the key ingredient to creating the depth of relationship and connection you desire.

So, return to the idea of pure potential. Think about a newborn in your life, whether it be your own child, a friend's baby, or a cousin. Whoever it is, think about how we came into the world without any of our stories. We came in without interpretations. We came in ready to see how our lives would unfold.

If you believe in past life or in utero experiences, that's fine. That's a different type of work. For the sake of this conversation I am talking about from day one, when you birthed into this life ready to rock. There's a newness there. A lightness. Freshness. And a time of hope. All over the world in any economic situation, you find a hopefulness, a joy, love, presence when a baby is born. So try to reconnect with your own pure potential. Even if it doesn't feel real to you in some way, trust me and go for it. You have wider potential than you have been living up to. And now you have the tools to get closer to actualizing that potential when it comes to your relationships. Remember, relationships are really the key to happiness in your personal life and success in your professional world as well.

You recommit moment to moment, day to day. This is the stuff that you will repeat again and again through this process. Fear will come up. Old stories will resurface over and over. Opportunities for new stories and interpretations will occur every day. Guilt will rear its ugly head. You'll want something, and you'll doubt your worth. And you will need to recommit again and again to your desire for connection, for that amazing feeling of love and trust and knowing.

That is what recommitment is all about. Deciding that your desire for connection is bigger than your fear. That the reward of intimacy is worth the risk of embarrassment or failure. When you're on this path of deep and meaningful relationships, you're clear that it's a commitment. You must be willing to let go of being right if it compromises the relationship, even when it's so damn tempting to dig your heels in and argue your point to the end. You have to want love and affinity more than you want to "win."

You muster up your courage. Courage, as we discussed earlier, is essential to creating deeper, meaningful, and fulfilling relationships, and therefore greater happiness in your life. Courage is required to be more open, vulnerable, and naked. Think about that first time you got naked in a romantic relationship. For many of us it was awkward at best, and terrifying at worst. But you wanted the reward of intimacy and pleasure. So, you found your courage and you got naked, literally. That's the mustering of courage you want to practice in your relationships.

I was talking to a client about her connections with the people in her life. She has friends, she has family, and people like her. Yet, she never felt truly supported. She wasn't really sure that she could be real in the community she had built around her. Would they really be there for her if she needed them? Did they really know her and like her? Did she really know them?

Her community seemed quite close, and she talked to people all the time, but she was engaging at a surface level. And it cost her. Sometimes the courage needed seems so small, but it stops us in our tracks because the fear *feels* so big.

And then her husband went out of town on work for an entire week, which was longer than she'd expected. She had two young children out of school for the summer. She felt bowled over, exhausted, and once again left to handle it all on her own. She was angry, frustrated, and upset, mainly directed at her husband.

However, most of what she was feeling was coming from her old stories and patterns. She had a story that she needed to handle everything on her own, that people let her down, that life was hard and treated her unfairly. She knew through our work together that this was a story that was no longer serving her.

However, when the time came to have a courageous conversation with her friends to ask for some support while her husband was gone, she faltered. We discussed her hesitation and discovered that the vulnerability required to ask a friend for a little help was terrifying to her. We talked about how she could make a really clear request that felt reasonable, yet a stretch for her. We practiced it together. I gave her a pep talk. And off she went into her life to be courageous out of her commitment to deepening her friendships and making her life better. Her friend was more than happy to say yes to her request, and now there's a window open for that friendship to deepen, to become more real and loving.

It's the everyday courage that will transform your relationships and ultimately transform your life.

You've got to go for it. You have to be willing to put yourself in the game. On the court. Participating full out. Because the thing about relationships is that they don't happen in isolation. They happen in relation to others. They can happen anywhere. They can happen when you're checking out at the grocery store and realize that it's the same checkout person that you see every week, so you pause and ask how her day is going. And you pause long enough to really hear her answer. Maybe you even throw in an appreciation for how friendly or efficient she always is. Relationship opportunities are around us all the time. There are micro-connections available to us every day, everywhere we go. You can practice everywhere.

Some relationships feel easier, and others require more courage. Sometimes you'll need to dig deep to find courage in the relationships where you're cultivating the next level of richer intimacy. Other times it may be that first exchange of vulnerability, the new friendship or romance, where the courage is needed. Either way, it's the same mindset and practices of naked communication that will carry you through with greater ease and connection.

You have to be willing to engage with others with the commitments of greater connection and deeper relationships everywhere you go in your life. When you start to relate to others that way as a habit, you'll find it gets easier and easier to connect more quickly and in a more fulfilling way. If you move into a new neighborhood or start a new job, you'll be able to build friendships within your communities. If you're longing to strengthen or restore the bonds with your current friends, partners, kids, or colleagues, you'll be able to reach out and connect with a fresh approach.

Look for opportunities to go for it! Every time I get off of a call with a client I leave them with fieldwork. The fieldwork is active practice toward their goals, dreams, or desired outcomes. The fieldwork is where the rubber meets the road. You can read this whole book, and have many breakthroughs and epiphanies, and I hope you have, but I want you to have more than fleeting insights. I want you to transform the way you relate to yourself and others so that you form deep and meaningful relationships throughout your life. That's the power of naked communication.

Start where you are. Make the first bold move toward connection, however small, and go for it. You want it. You deserve it. And now you are really capable of it.

Lastly, sprinkle compassion like freaking fairy dust all over this process.

Compassion for yourself, first and foremost. The idea of being your own worst critic is often true. The crap you say to yourself, about yourself, in your head is damaging to your connection with your spirit. At the risk of sounding woo woo, love and forgive the hell out of yourself. When you're feeling good about yourself it's so much easier for others to connect with you. It also feels a hell of a lot better than being stuck in the endless feedback loop of self-judgment. Show yourself the same compassion you would show a beloved friend.

Then, find some compassion for the people around you. For the shared human experience. We're all inherently complex and flawed. We're perfectly imperfect. We get our feelings hurt. We react. We bring our old stories into our present conversations. We're doing the best we can with the skills we have, and screwing up and cleaning up along the way.

We're also divinely capable of love, connection, and deep relationship. It's one of the most beautiful things about being human. We're born with a capacity and a longing for love and connection. To attach. To bond. To be in relationship. To have shared experiences. To not walk alone. To laugh together. To cry together. To bolster each other when shit is hard.

But we have to be willing to find compassion when we, or others, mess up. Compassion isn't about letting people off the hook. It's not about thinking what they did was right. When you can find compassion, you're a step closer to finding forgiveness. To letting go, so you can have more freedom and space to get back in the game and strengthen your relationships.

I'm not saying you have to stay in a relationship with someone whom you don't want to be in relationship with. If a relationship consistently causes you pain or depletes you even with all of your "naked" skills in play, you'll want to explore whether or not it's worth the energy to maintain it. Only you can know which relationships truly serve you and your best self in the world. With naked communication, you can leave relationships as cleanly and compassionately as possible, honoring the connection that was once there even if it's time to let it go.

You can use naked communication as you forge new relationships, sustain long-term relationships, and say goodbye to completed relationships. Being clean, clear, and compassionate in all of your conversations, all your array of daily communications, can become an integral part of who you are.

With practice, commitment, and support you are capable of building and sustaining deep, lasting interpersonal relationships with infinite amounts of people in various environments throughout your life.

Truly, you are that powerful.

You have that capacity for love. You are that deserving of happiness. You are that courageous.

You came into the world naked, and thus to naked you return. Pure potential. Endless possibility. Unlimited love. Boundless community. Real connection. Deep relationships.

And when you stumble, go back and try again. You're human, doing the best you can with the skills you have. But, *you're* extra awesome, because you're practicing new and better skills *all the time.* You're living naked.

Conclusion

*"Do you have the courage to bring forth
the treasures that are hidden within you?"*
—Elizabeth Gilbert

Yes. Yes, I believe you do.

Thank you for courageously stepping into this journey with me. The world is yearning for deep connection, for a shared experience of love and understanding. You are now a part of that possibility. It is unusual for people to dive into their own growth and transformation. It is a bold and courageous act to explore who you are and how you can evolve. So, thank you. Thank you for being that awesome. For reading all the way to here and peeling away your layers. For getting naked with me.

I know that your relationships are the key to your personal happiness and professional success. I know you want yours to be extraordinary and that you're now ready to make that happen in a big and beautiful way in your life. I'm so, so psyched for you and the lucky people who are in your community and get to be in your naked orbit.

Because here's the thing. **Naked communication is much bigger than just you and your loved ones.** It goes out in a wave of impact, as more and more people feel heard, seen, and valued for who they are and what they bring to the world. As more people are able to press pause on judgment, seek out their innate desire to build meaningful relationships, share themselves honestly in spite of fear— the more love and connection is possible in our communities and even on a global scale.

That is the power of the work you've embarked on with naked communication. **The possibility of more love and connection on the planet.** And, yes, I'm an eternal optimist. But, I'm not naive. I've seen lots of the world, talked to people from many backgrounds, experienced my own challenges and suffering. I know it's not all "peace, dude" and everything is copacetic and harmonious.

And yet, I choose optimism. I choose connection. I choose to put relationships first. I choose to speak up, to share myself, to be curious, to find courage, to seek out compassion, to be as naked as possible as often as possible.

And now you're choosing that adventure with me, for which I (and the world) have deep gratitude.

Remember, this is not a one and done scenario. You don't just read a book and your life is forever changed without any further effort or reflection. Naked communication is a lifelong commitment and journey. Please, please don't berate yourself if you forget and find yourself in a messy argument with your partner or friend. We humans are messy, lovely, amazing beings.

Get back in your naked zone, reread parts of the book where you need to polish up your practice, clean up the mess you got tangled in, and let compassion pour over you so you can move on. This is a life. A beautifully connected, deeply loving, wildly courageous, and sometimes messy life. Naked is clean, clear, courageous, and compassionate. It takes time and practice to integrate all those pieces into the fiber of your being consistently over time.

You're well on your way. Let this be your new beginning. Let this be the exciting moment, standing on the edge of a big adventure.

And, be sure to take advantage of the supports I've put together for you. This is not a solo journey, and I truly want to know how it's going for you. It helps me support you better if I know where the challenges are, where things weren't clear, and where the big celebrations are happening in your lives. Below are all the ways you can stay in touch with me and get the most out of this book.

Join our amazing community of folks who are changing their lives and changing the world.

1. Grab your free book companion guide to the book at www.sagebhobbs.com/bookguide. It'll help with that whole "inspiration *and* participation get you the results you desire" thing I've said over and over again. It's designed to support you in a really clear way, with reflection activities and worksheets that go hand-in-hand with the book so you can put it all to use in your life and relationships.

2. Are you having relationship breakthroughs? Challenges? Big ahas? I'd love to hear how it's going for you. You can reach out to me with your stories and insights on naked communication at sage@sagebhobbs.com. And if you want to want to know how we can together because you're ready to accelerate your results and focus on building awesome relationships, you can do that too. Many people need more than a book to keep them in action. I know I do.

3. On social media you can see behind the scenes of how I used naked communication in my own life as a mom, wife, and a woman in the world.
    https://www.facebook.com/sagebhobbs/
    https://www.instagram.com/sagebhobbs/

Naked communication works when you really make a commitment to using it. It's not always easy, but the results are amazing. Not only do your relationships feel better, but *you* feel better because you're living a more courageous and expressive life. You feel more vibrant and alive. Others want to be around people with that confident and radiant energy. Welcome to the naked communication tribe. Thank you for jumping in.

Get your naked on.

Much love and loads of courage,
Sage

Acknowledgments

I could write an entire book acknowledging the people in my life who have gotten me here, truly. I feel so excited and honored to share my deep gratitude for them, and it still won't begin to capture how much their support, encouragement, and love have meant to me.

My family. I had the ridiculous good fortune to be granted the best parents in the world. They shared lessons and values I didn't even know were extraordinary, but have profoundly shaped who I am and who I hope to be. Such as: make a difference with your life. Your contribution to the world is important. Love fiercely, forgive regularly. See the world, explore, ask questions, be curious. Possibilities are endless, so don't get boxed in. And, laugh often, dance your ass off, and have FUN! While my dad is no longer here in body, I truly felt him by my side every step of this process. And thank goodness, because if I have even one small part of him in me then I am profoundly lucky.

Nathan, there are no words for how I hit the partner-in-life jackpot when I met you. Somehow you manage to be everything I ever needed. Kind, funny, smart, sexy, strong, and deeply loving. And, you totally support me in my big, wild, anything-is possible dreams, no matter how out there they may sometimes be. I would never be fully me without you.

My kids, oh my kids. These two little humans trust me to guide them and love them, even when I royally screw up. I can't believe how patient they are with me. Never have I been more humbled than by being a parent. Never have I been more grateful than becoming a mom. D and J, I love you to the moon and back.

My amazingly creative brother, Luke, who reminds me that following our passion is important. My generous and courageous sister, Chloe, who is wise beyond her years and makes me strive to be as cool as she thinks I am. My 93-year-old grandparents, who drop crazy pearls of wisdom on me every time we speak. My aunts, uncles, cousins, steps, and in-laws who've always made me feel loved and welcomed, and who make me feel so lucky to be part of a big, beautiful family.

My friends, my cheerleaders, my soul sisters. We've laughed our asses off and cried our eyes out. We've been though falling in and out of love. Through giving and losing of life. We've talked for countless (literally) hours about our dreams and plans. Thank you, Katie Morris, Erica Barth, Christi Gubser, Doria Sutton, Martine Conway, Irene Balakrishnan, Diane Jensen, Katie Douglas, Jill Winkler Douglas, Sanam Roder, Margaret Riedel, and so many more amazing women whom I've been lucky to have in my life. My UCD girls, neighbors, childhood friends, former colleagues, S. 42nd Street college crew: many thanks and much love for being *the* most badass and brilliant women on the planet, for reals. And for all the ways you've supported me, from pep talks to childcare to early readings of this book and to endless listening to my ideas. You women give me faith in humanity.

My mentors, guides, and support crew. I've been lucky enough to know some of my mentors and guides personally, and others I've learned from afar, but all of you have made a difference in who I am and how I aim to live my life. Kim Johnson, for constantly getting me out of my own head. Parrish Wilson and Michelle Asakawa, for nurturing this work into a more beautiful form. Alex Honeysett, for your sweet encouragement and kickass marketing advice. Robbyn Fernandez, for being an example of a smart, strong working mom and believing in me from the get-go. Jane Goldstone, for showing me how to be a badass, with courage and freedom, when I needed the reminder. Laura Kupperman, Kelly Elle Kenworthy, and Wendy DeRosa for being on this wild ride together, out to spread our work with the world. Jill Sessa, my techie goddess, for helping me sleep better knowing certain things are handled magically by you.

Marie Forleo, for being the brilliant, elegant, fierce, Jersey girl that first showed me what this whole biz thing could look like in the real world. Danielle LaPorte, whose writing speaks directly to my soul and makes me underline nearly every line. Michael Franti, whose "let me see you jumpin'!" energy is so captivating that I feel wildly ALIVE and want to marry my work with changing the world too.

And most importantly, YOU. Naked communicator friends both new and old. Some of your stories are shared within this work, for which I am so grateful. Thank you for reading, for engaging, for peeling back the layers, for going for it. YOU are the most important part of this big, amazing, life-changing adventure.

About the Author

Sage B. Hobbs is a coach, author, and speaker who is known for her direct, insightful, and compassionate approach to communication and personal growth.

She's worked with thousands of individuals and groups for more than 15 years to both transform their relationships and increase their personal fulfillment.

Sage deeply believes that our happiness and success are directly related to the quality of our relationships, *and* that it's possible to create the fulfilling relationships we really want. She's been a student of transformational work all of her life (literally), and brings her enthusiasm, wisdom, and relentless optimism to everything she does.

Prior to creating her current work on naked communication, Sage received her bachelor's degree from the University of Pennsylvania, her master's degree from the University of Colorado Denver, and spent a decade working with teens and families to navigate the wild path of growing up.

She's also a mom of two, a cancer survivor, a proud teacher's wife, a "retired" school counselor, a world traveler, and a book lover. You can often find her dancing in her kitchen, cleaning up a kid's mess (while cursing under her breath), moving on her yoga mat, lifting her face toward the sun for a hit of happiness, or on the phone dishing out real and loving guidance to one of the many women in her world.

A Philly girl at heart, she now lives in beautiful Boulder, Colorado, with her favorite man on earth, Nathan, and their two awesome kids.